How to Open & Operate a Financially Successful

Personal Chef

Business

By Carla Rowley and Lee Rowley

HOW TO OPEN & OPERATE A FINANCIALLY SUCCESSFUL PERSONAL CHEF BUSINESS — WITH COMPANION CD-ROM

ISBN-13: 978-1-60138-141-5   ISBN-10: 1-60138-141-7
Library of Congress Cataloging-in-Publication Data

Rowley, Carla, 1977-
  How to open & operate a financially successful personal chef business
/ by Carla Rowley and Lee Rowley.
      p. cm.
  Includes bibliographical references and index.
  ISBN-13: 978-1-60138-141-5 (alk. paper)
  ISBN-10: 1-60138-141-7 (alk. paper)
  1. Food service management. 2. Cooks. 3. Entrepreneurship. I.
Rowley, Lee, 1973- II. Title.

  TX911.3.M27R69 2008
  647.95068--dc22
                            2008028007

INTERIOR LAYOUT DESIGN: Nicole Deck ndeck@atlantic-pub.com

COVER PHOTO PROVIDED BY: Chef Jaime Miller • Remember That Chef • In Home Dining & Personal Chef Services • 905-560-6924 • Fax: 905-560-9795 • www.rememberthatchef.ca • jaime@rememberthatchef.ca

Printed in the United States

We recently lost our beloved pet "Bear," who was not only our best and dearest friend but also the "Vice President of Sunshine" here at Atlantic Publishing. He did not receive a salary but worked tirelessly 24 hours a day to please his parents. Bear was a rescue dog that turned around and showered myself, my wife Sherri, his grandparents Jean, Bob and Nancy and every person and animal he met (maybe not rabbits) with friendship and love. He made a lot of people smile every day.

We wanted you to know that a portion of the profits of this book will be donated to The Humane Society of the United States.

–Douglas & Sherri Brown

THE HUMANE SOCIETY
OF THE UNITED STATES ©

The human-animal bond is as old as human history. We cherish our animal companions for their unconditional affection and acceptance. We feel a thrill when we glimpse wild creatures in their natural habitat or in our own backyard.

Unfortunately, the human-animal bond has at times been weakened. Humans have exploited some animal species to the point of extinction.

The Humane Society of the United States makes a difference in the lives of animals here at home and worldwide. The HSUS is dedicated to creating a world where our relationship with animals is guided by compassion. We seek a truly humane society in which animals are respected for their intrinsic value, and where the human-animal bond is strong.

Want to help animals? We have plenty of suggestions. Adopt a pet from a local shelter, join The Humane Society and be a part of our work to help companion animals and wildlife. You will be funding our educational, legislative, investigative and outreach projects in the U.S. and across the globe.

Or perhaps you'd like to make a memorial donation in honor of a pet, friend or relative? You can through our Kindred Spirits program. And if you'd like to contribute in a more structured way, our Planned Giving Office has suggestions about estate planning, annuities, and even gifts of stock that avoid capital gains taxes.

Maybe you have land that you would like to preserve as a lasting habitat for wildlife. Our Wildlife Land Trust can help you. Perhaps the land you want to share is a backyard—that's enough. Our Urban Wildlife Sanctuary Program will show you how to create a habitat for your wild neighbors.

So you see, it's easy to help animals. And The HSUS is here to help.

The Humane Society of the United States
2100 L Street NW
Washington, DC 20037
202-452-1100
www.hsus.org

Table of Contents

Foreword...9

Introduction 13

Chapter 1: What is a Personal Chef? 19
The Growing Need for Personal Chefs............................19
What Does a Personal Chef Do? 22
What Qualities Does a Successful
Personal Chef Need? 25
Where Does a Personal Chef Work?................................27
What Areas Can a Personal Chef Specialize In?............28
Who Hires Personal Chefs? 31

Chapter 2: What Education is Required
to Become a Personal Chef? 33
Do You Need a Formalized Education?............................33
What Are My Culinary Education Options?....................35
The Culinary Business Academy 38
Business Education and Experience 39

Chapter 3: Developing a Business Plan 45

Why Do I Need a Business Plan?............................45

The Elements of a Business Plan............................48

Chapter 4: Setting Up a Business Budget...........83

Chapter 5: What Equipment Does a Personal Chef Need?............................91

Chapter 6: Where Should I Set Up My Business?...99

Working in Your Client's Kitchen............................99

Cooking in Your Own Kitchen............................103

Renting a Kitchen Space............................106

What to Consider When Determining Where You Will Work............................109

Chapter 7: Hiring and Training Employees...........111

Finding and Pre-Screening Employees............................111

The Interview Process............................119

Training Employees............................126

Contracting with Professionals............................128

Chapter 8: Catering to the Dietary Needs of Your Clients............................131

Health Related Eating Restrictions............................132

Religious and Culturally Based Dietary Needs............................139

Vegetarian and Vegan Diets............................141

Diets and Weight Loss..143

Chapter 9: Learning to Cater to Your Client's Personal Preferences 145

Chapter 10: Customer Service and Satisfaction.................................155
Creating a Customer Friendly Business 156
What Do I Do When One of My Clients Ends Service?.162
Customer Service Do's and Don'ts..................................164
Turning Unhappy Customers into Happy Customers..172
Asking for Referrals...177

Chapter 11: What Should You Charge? 181
Overhead and Other Expenses...183
Credentials, Level of Expertise, and Experience 186
Specialty Services 187
Competition in Your Area...187
Demand in Your Area...188
Developing Fees for Your Personal Chef Services..........189

Chapter 12: Preparing for the Financial Responsibilities of Being Self-Employed...........193
Leaving Your Current Job to Enter the World
of the Business Owner..193
Benefits and Insurance 197

Chapter 13: Marketing Your Personal Chef Services 201

Internet Marketing: Bringing your
Business to the Web 202
Techniques to Avoid When Using
Keywords in Your Web Site Content 217
Other Ways to Use Keywords to Improve
Your Search Engine Rankings 222

Chapter 14: Software and Web Services to Help You Run Your Personal Chef Business 229

Web Site Creation Tools 230
CGI Forms and Autoresponder Tools 238
Visitor Tracking Software 243
Accounting, Business, and Financial Tools 250

Chapter 15: Case Studies 257

Bibliography 263

Dedication & Biography 264

Glossary 265

Index 287

Foreword

By Deborah J. DuBost

In today's environment, where families are fast-forwarding through life with busy careers and a plentitude of after-school activities, more and more people are choosing to hire personal or private chefs to fulfill the need for a home cooked meal. While just a decade ago, services like this were typically used by only the wealthy, today, many everyday families are deciding to hire personal chefs to cook nutritional, well-balanced meals. As the temptation to grab dinner from a fast-food restaurant on the way home from work or from picking up kids from soccer practice increases, so does the guilt for not providing your family with a meal that serves their best interests. For these "families-on-the-go," the services of a personal chef can be invaluable and can provide a tasty, but also healthy, alternative to fast-food or prepackaged, frozen meals.

With the need for these services increasing, deciding to open a personal or private chef business can not only be a rewarding personal experience, but a smart business investment as well. Becoming a personal or private chef allows you to take part in an activity that you enjoy – cooking – and also to escape the typical restaurant environment that most chefs are accustom to. Opening your own business allows you the freedom to express your own creativity and to show off your expertise with a specific style of cooking. As an owner, you can operate the business to align with your own personal and creative vision.

Not only does becoming a personal or private chef give you personal freedom, but it may also give you the financial freedom that you always imagined for yourself and was never available as a chef in a restaurant. According to the U.S. Department of Labor, providing professional personal chef services is one of the fastest growing segments of the food service business. Personal chefs can expect to make between $100 and $400 a day.

How to Open & Operate a Financially Successful Personal Chef Business: With Companion CD-ROM is a complete guide for anyone thinking of starting down the path of entrepreneurship. The book provides detailed, easy to read information on what it takes to become a personal or private chef, what type of education is typically required, and basic business operation information, such as writing a business plan, setting up a budget for your new business, and the different options on locations for operating your business. The book even contains a CD-ROM which has a fully customizable sample business plan and all the forms and checklists located throughout the book. Authors Carla and Lee Rowley also offer specific catering information such as selecting menus that fit the health, nutrition, and religious needs of your clients, the importance of learning your clients' food preferences, and specific customer service advice.

As a personal caterer myself, I can attest that this book is a must-have for all experienced chefs looking to start their own personal chef business. My company, Let's Party and Catering, offers personal chef services right in the client's home. During our sessions, we educate our clients on the nutritional aspects of the meal and, at the end of preparation, we pack all of the extra food into freezable containers for the client's enjoyment at a later time. Our Private Chef services are set for group dinners of two or more, and can also be set as a Culinary Class for the attendees; where the recipes are provided and prepared by the guests. This book is a great introduction into not only the world of a personal chef, but also into opening a successful, financially stable new business. Opening any new business is a huge undertaking, but with your own creative motivation and *How to Open & Operate a Financially Successful Personal Chef Business* you are sure to have all the inspiration and information that you need to start your business off on the right path. Good luck with your business endeavors and happy cooking!

Deborah J. DuBost
Owner/Executive Chef, Let's Party & Catering
www.LetsPartyandCatering.com
letsparty_catering@hotmail.com
386-216-7651

Born in Washington, D.C., Deborah DuBost moved to Merritt Island, Florida in 1965. DuBost worked at Disney World's Magic Kingdom under the guidance of Executive Chef Klaus Friesendorf at Top of the World Restaurant as his Prep & Sous Chef. DuBost graduated from The University of Texas at Austin in 1978 with a Bachelor of Science degree in Nursing. After graduation, DuBost made her way back to Florida when she was hired by Southern Bell Telephone Company. In 1998, DuBost retired from AT&T Communications. With her love of the culinary arts always in the back of her mind, she graduated from Johnson & Wales' College of Culinary Arts. Let's Party and Catering opened in 2003 and today, five years later, DuBost feels as if she has learned many lessons along the path of entrepreneurship and has gained some of the best customers around.

 # Let's Party and Catering

Introduction

Do you enjoy cooking and baking, and consider these activities an escape from the everyday world? Do you spend every possible minute in the kitchen, creating delicious treats for your family and guests? Do you delight in each compliment and each recipe request you receive from people who have tasted your unique creations?

If you can answer yes to these questions, you have probably thought at one time or another about turning your love for cooking into a full-time career. If you are like many people, though, the prospect of transitioning into a career in cooking might seem daunting. How would you get clients? How would you come up with the money to start your business? What types of food would you make, and whom would you serve?

Unfortunately, too many talented people face these questions and, lacking the resources or support to find the answers, never let themselves explore the prospect of a career in the culinary arts.

This book might be just the resource and the support you have been hoping for.

If you are passionate about cooking, and have always wanted to cook for a living, the information contained in this book could prove to be some of the most valuable information you will ever read. Within these pages, you will learn how to plan a personal chef business and begin taking the steps to achieve the career you have always dreamed of.

A career as a personal chef can be a perfect solution for people who love to cook, but who are not excited about any of the traditional careers available to people in the culinary arts.

Many chefs who are not aware of the emerging personal chef opportunities that have become available in recent years feel that they are limited to the constraints of cooking in a restaurant owned by someone else. Although working in this type of environment might pay the bills, it can sometimes limit your creativity and leave you feeling unchallenged. Working for a restaurateur also significantly limits a chef's income – unless you are willing to move each time a more lucrative opportunity becomes available at another restaurant, your income is limited to what the owner is willing to pay you.

Another option pursued by many chefs is to open their own restaurant. Although this is a dream shared by many people in the culinary arts, opening a restaurant takes a huge financial investment and often requires taking out enormous loans to finance the restaurant space, pay your staff members, purchase ingredients and supplies, and market the restaurant to local diners. Furthermore, new restaurants often take several years before a profit is even made. Because of these challenges, many chefs are left deterred by the prospect of undertaking such a large financial investment that will take so long to show any financial return.

A private chef works for one client exclusively, to meet their tastes and needs. Because a private chef is limited to one customer or organization and is employed exclusively for that person or organization, he or she is limited to the needs of that client. A private chef might prepare and serve up to three meals a day for the client. Although it can provide long-term job stability, it is easy for a private chef to become bored in this career; once a private chef knows how to cater to the needs of his or her client, he or she can feel that this career lacks the challenges necessary to maintain his or her passion for food.

A personal chef works with various families and organizations and has no exclusive contract limiting his or her services to just one client or organization. Starting a personal chef business provides an option that offers an opportunity for a chef to open a business with a significantly lower financial investment than opening a restaurant and affords the chef the ability to be creative and constantly challenged.

In today's busy society, the need for personal chefs is growing day by day. The career, social, and family demands placed upon people today have created a unique need for the expert services of personal chefs who can take care of the often time-consuming task of preparing and serving meals. Busy families that want to have nutritional meals but do not have time to cook, elderly people with specific dietary needs who find it increasingly difficult to cook for themselves, and individuals and families that entertain and host dinner parties often, but do not have the time to cook for large groups, are all potential clients for personal chefs. This book addresses the unique needs of all types of customers, including the difficult customer, and how to cater to their personal needs.

As you might have guessed, it takes more than just the ability to cook to be successful as a personal chef. Although cooking nutritional and tasty meals is imperative to success as a personal chef, there are many business aspects that must also be explored and carefully planned for. As with any business, there are many mistakes that a new businessperson can make; these mistakes can cost you thousands of dollars in lost profit and can ultimately cost you your success in the culinary field. The purpose of this book is to give you the tools to troubleshoot potential business pitfalls and be prepared to make your business profitable and successful.

In the following pages, you will learn what a personal chef is, what a personal chef does, and what valuable business tools you will need for success. You need not have a degree in business to learn how to operate and run a personal chef business. However, as with any business venture, it is important to develop the business savvy necessary to reach your potential customers, make wise business and financial decisions, keep your customers happy, and generate repeat business.

In the following chapters, we will take a journey through every aspect of a personal chef business. You will learn, in detail, what kinds of tasks a personal chef undertakes and what kinds of different settings a personal chef works in. You will also learn how to build a business plan, undertake any necessary education, procure the equipment and supplies necessary to create and package meals for your clients, work with your customers to identify their needs, account for their dietary preferences and restrictions, and above all, keep them happy. You will also learn various marketing techniques that you can use to reach your ideal customers.

Grab a pen and paper because you might want to take notes as you read through this book and learn the secrets to success as a personal chef. Make yourself comfortable and prepare to dive into the life of a personal chef.

What is a Personal Chef?

Before we begin exploring how to open and run a successful personal chef business, let us explore why people would choose to use a personal chef to prepare meals and examine what a personal chef is and does in more detail.

In this chapter, you will learn about the activities of a personal chef and understand why this service is essential for many families today. You will also learn about the importance of specializing in certain cuisines or diets and identify some of the personal and professional traits that can help make you a successful personal chef. This will help you make sure that a career as a personal chef is right for you and help you prepare to enter the world of personal chef service.

The Growing Need for Personal Chefs

The popularity of using personal chefs to provide ready-to-eat meals has increased dramatically as families have become busier and have begun taking on obligations that were unheard of a few decades ago.

In today's society, it is not uncommon for both spouses to balance career and family, in addition to social obligations and other tasks. Working adults find it more difficult than ever to find enough time to meet all of their obligations.

Single-parent families are also becoming more common, with one parent acting as the sole breadwinner, homework help expert, and chauffeur of the household. After a long day of dropping the children off at school, spending the day at work, and running the kids to after-school activities and little league practice, it is difficult for working adults to find the time and energy to create home cooked meals at all, let alone ones that are low fat, nutritionally balanced, and full of fresh ingredients.

As a result, many families end up resorting to fast food meals that they can simply pick up on the way home from work. Others rely on pre-packaged frozen entrees that can be thrown in the oven. Although these types of meals are quick solutions for busy parents who need to feed themselves and their children on the go, the foods that comprise these meals generally lack nutritional value, contain ingredients that are detrimental to the health of the parents and children, and add fuel to the obesity epidemic sweeping across the United States and many other developed countries.

As a personal chef, you can provide a much healthier alternative that is convenient, quick, and simple for the family on the go to heat and eat. Imagine how valuable you can be to busy families as a personal chef by providing tasty, nutritional alternatives to fast food fare and frozen meals that have sat in the supermarket freezer case for an undeterminable length of time.

By lending your expertise to busy families as a personal chef, you can provide your customer with an invaluable service by using your knowledge, experience, and passion for food to provide them with delicious meals for each week.

Many personal chefs add even more value to their culinary services by specializing in various cuisines and dietary needs to best use their strengths as a chef. This also helps build a sustainable business, because they can attract a niche segment of the people who need the services of a personal chef. Specializing also gives you more opportunity to create the types of food you enjoy creating the most, which can significantly increase your career satisfaction and attract clients who appreciate your enthusiasm and passion.

It is important to remember when starting a personal chef business that you have room to be creative and to make the business meet your own personal vision. No two personal chefs are alike, and your creativity is a factor that will help you retain your clients and receive referrals for new clients. Although this book will give you a blueprint for launching and building your personal chef business, it is important that you work with the ideas in this book and modify them as necessary to complement your personal culinary vision, so you can begin to create the business of your dreams.

What Does a Personal Chef Do?

A personal chef creates meals that are ready for his or her clients to eat when they return home after work, school, and other obligations. A personal chef may also create meals that are packaged and refrigerated or frozen so clients can simply heat the meals and have them on the dinner table in a matter of minutes.

A personal chef works closely with his or her clients to provide tasty and nutritional meals that meet the clients' personal needs and tastes. One way personal chefs make sure their clients are satisfied is to frequently communicate with the clients to form and adjust meal plans. Asking for input and suggestions from customers is one of the best ways to maintain long-term client relationships, not only because you will be better able to cater to their preferences, but because your clients will appreciate the fact that you have their best interests in mind when planning and preparing their meals. You might also have to conduct significant research on particular diets, health conditions, or religious beliefs to be able to cater to the clients' specialized tastes and needs.

Many personal chefs cook the meals in the clients' kitchens and package them so they can be frozen and reheated at the client's meal time. Meals are typically packaged with detailed instructions so clients only have to follow minimal preparation requirements to complete the meal. Many clients appreciate this arrangement for two reasons: first, because they know where the meal was prepared – some people who need personal chef services have reservations about eating meals that are prepared in the chef's home, because they do not have the opportunity to make sure the cooking environment is sanitary; second, because when they sit down to dinner, they will not have to worry about having you in their house – this gives the clients the ability to have some private time with their families.

A personal chef differs from a private chef because he or she works for multiple clients rather than being limited to one client. A personal chef can also offer his or her services for a much more affordable price than a private chef. The result is a chef service that is accessible and appealing to more customers. This is because a personal chef can provide professionally prepared meals at a price that is affordable to the average person and still provide customers with the luxury of professionally prepared meals.

As a personal chef, you will also be required to take into consideration your clients' specific dietary needs and restrictions and to select ingredients for your clients' meals based on those needs and restrictions. We will talk more in depth about this in Chapter 9.

Personal chefs can also provide cooking classes in the client's home or in the community. In addition to giving you extra income, this service can help establish you as a culinary authority in your community. Conducting classes is also a good way to obtain referrals for your personal chef services because attendees who enjoy your classes will want their families and friends to experience your culinary genius as well.

Some chefs choose to specialize in either catering for special events or providing meals for several different customers. No matter what the event or whom you are working with, it is important to establish a meal plan with each customer.

Establishing a meal plan and reviewing it with your client helps to ensure that you, as the personal chef, are providing the types of food and variety that your customer desires. This can be especially helpful in getting to know a new client's preferences and expectations.

It is imperative that you learn about any religious or health-related dietary restrictions or food allergies your client might have. Sometimes a client is unfamiliar with every ingredient that makes up a specific dish and might not realize that the food they are allergic to is included in their entree. Some food allergies are potentially fatal. It is imperative that you avoid using ingredients that could cause your client to have an allergic reaction.

After you set up the meal plans, they should be submitted to the client for approval. Once the meals are approved, the chef will complete the shopping for all food items involved and will prepare the food for the client, usually in the client's own kitchen.

Taking time to create a detailed list before going to the store will prevent you from having to improvise or make an emergency trip to the store. This is especially important if you will be using your client's kitchen because you will have a limited amount of time to prepare the food. Being prepared is also critical to managing your time, especially as your clientele grows.

If you are working with several families on an ongoing

basis, often you will go to the client's home once a week – or once every other week – and prepare the meals in the client's kitchen. The meals will then be available for the client to heat and eat at their desired meal time. Be sure to familiarize yourself with the client's kitchen before showing up to prepare your first batch of meals.

It might be helpful for you to provide your client with a comment card each week. Comment cards are a quick and convenient way for your clients to provide feedback on your services.

What Qualities Does a Successful Personal Chef Need?

As with any profession, a personal chef career is not right for everyone. A personal chef must possess, or cultivate, certain traits in order to be successful. If you have a passion for cooking and truly desire to be a personal chef, any of these traits can be learned and developed.

One of these traits is the love and passion for food. A successful personal chef must love to cook and bring life to their food. Many clients who hire a personal chef are passionate about food, but do not have the time to prepare food that lives up to their expectations. A good personal chef recognizes the client's passion for food and uses his or her ability to cook with creativity and flair to make each meal a culinary adventure.

Another trait a personal chef must possess, or develop, is people skills. Although one of the many advantages to having a personal chef business is the freedom to be creative, the customer must always come first. A good personal chef always listens to the customer's wants and needs and does their absolute best to provide an outstanding meal for each client. If you do not always agree with a client's ideas or suggestions, learn to compromise and offer solutions.

A personal chef must be creative and develop their own recipes and dishes to fit the client's individual preferences and needs. Some clients will be harder to please than others. As a personal chef, you must always act professionally. Always listen to your client's concerns and be prepared to offer solutions. Ask for feedback and accept constructive criticism to keep your clients happy and build your clientele.

As a personal chef, it is imperative that you listen to your clients. Provide a questionnaire or sit down with the client and make notes about the client's personal needs and expectations. If the client is unhappy with a meal, it is important to listen to what the client did and did not like and work out a solution to prevent repeating the mistake. Always submit meal plans in a timely manner so your clients will have adequate time to review and approve the menu. Some clients will be more difficult to please than others.

Another important trait a personal chef must either have or develop is excellent time-management skills. As a personal chef, you will be working on your own, with no boss to hold you accountable or time clock to punch. Although this might seem appealing to you, it is important to remain disciplined and manage your time effectively. Time management will become even more important as you grow your business and take on more clients.

Where Does a Personal Chef Work?

Many personal chefs work in the kitchens of their clients, rather than preparing meals in their own kitchens. Most chefs set up a time with their client and go to the client's house once a week or once every other week and prepare the food in the client's kitchen. This eliminates the need for transporting finished entrees and reduces the chance of food getting destroyed, damaged, or contaminated in transit.

Cooking in your client's kitchen does pose some difficulties. Sometimes, clients may not have the items you need to prepare a certain dish. It also might be difficult to locate items in an unfamiliar kitchen. Ask your client to give you a tour of their kitchen before your first cooking appointment. Also, create a portable kitchen kit that contains critical items that your client may not own. Your client is probably not a professional chef himself and probably does not have every item that a culinary expert views as critical in preparing a meal.

Some personal chefs prefer to cook in their own kitchens and deliver the food to the client. This eliminates the need to transport equipment. Another major advantage to using your own kitchen is that you do not have to familiarize yourself with each client's kitchen. Transporting the food to your client's home does, however, provide the need for a business vehicle large enough to safely transport items.

As we mentioned earlier, it also provides the risk of food becoming damaged, destroyed, or contaminated while in transit.

If your intention is to build a larger business, hire employees, and specialize in catering, you might want to consider renting a kitchen space. Renting a space will provide more room for multiple employees to work at the same time. Renting a space will also provide extra room for meeting with customers who want to sample your product before contracting your services.

As with choosing to cook in your own kitchen, renting a space will also require a proper vehicle in which to safely transport food items. Renting a space also involves more expense and overhead because you will be paying for the space.

When choosing where you want to work, consider your needs and specialties. No one option is best for everyone. If you want to keep your practice somewhat small, working in your own kitchen or your client's kitchen may be the better way to go. But, if you want to provide a place to meet with your clients and provide samplings of your work or you envision a larger business with multiple employees, renting a larger area could be the way to go.

What Areas Can a Personal Chef Specialize In?

As a personal chef, you are your own boss, so your possibilities of specialization are virtually endless. You have the freedom to specialize to meet your passions. Specializing also allows you to target a more specific market that is looking for your specific service and variety.

One area of specialization is catering. You can choose to cater for large or small groups. You can also target your marketing to reach either organizations or families. You can provide your catering services for weddings, small dinner parties, corporate banquets, anniversary parties, or reunions.

The catering business is one of the fastest growing areas in the food service industry. The more you build your reputation as a caterer, the more demand you will be in. The best news is that you need not limit yourself to just catering. Some personal chefs choose to work as personal chefs in their client's homes as well as provide catering services on a case-by-case basis.

When beginning your personal chef business, you can also choose to specialize in working with clients with specific dietary needs. Clients with health-restricted diets, such as diabetes and high blood pressure, require a special diet to maintain their health and well-being. Perhaps you have specific health-related dietary restrictions of your own or have had to cook for a family member who has had dietary restrictions. Your expertise and specialization can place you in high demand for those who need help in the kitchen but might be fearful that a personal chef will not understand or adhere to their specific dietary needs. You can also use your expertise in this area to provide food that is not lacking in flavor.

If you have a specific ethnic food that you are passionate

about cooking, consider specializing in that food. Your expertise will appeal to clients who are either of that ethnicity and prefer to eat familiar foods, or who particularly enjoy the type of ethnic food you specialize in. If you feel limited by choosing one ethnic food and have a special talent with several types of ethnic food, you can choose to specialize in each of your favorite ethnic foods.

If you are a vegetarian or vegan, you might feel limited by the vegetarian and vegan food options currently available at your local restaurants. If you like to experiment with creating flavorful foods that are vegetarian and vegan, a specialization in vegetarian and vegan meals would give you the opportunity to provide tasty vegetarian and vegan meals to your clientele. In turn, you would appeal to your clientele by offering them flavor-filled vegetarian and vegan meals that personal chefs who primarily cook with meat and animal products could not provide.

If you like to teach others how to cook, you could specialize in providing cooking lessons. These lessons can be in the client's home or can be scheduled by the chef and open to the public at the location the chef chooses. These cooking lessons can be tailored to your personal specialties and expertise and can help you meet potential clients in the community.

With a significant segment of the population becoming increasingly health conscious, many clients are interested in organic diets. Some clients, although wanting an organic diet, do not know where to begin. A chef who specializes in organic foods and already has expertise is invaluable to these clients. If you choose organic foods as your specialty, you can take the burden off your clients by shopping for organic foods and preparing these foods to maximize taste and flavor. Organic foods are sometimes hard to find and are costly. With your expertise, you can cut the client's food cost by researching organic food suppliers and finding the best price for organic foods.

Perhaps your passion is preparing low-fat, low-calorie meals that are tasty but do not pack on extra pounds. With the growing obesity epidemic in the United States, many people wish to lose extra pounds, but do not want to sacrifice taste. Many pre-packaged diet entrees and foods provided by diet plans lack taste. Many of these meals are also small in portion size, leaving the consumer hungry. By using your specialty to create flavor-filled food in reasonably sized portions, you are not only feeding your passion for cooking but offering your clients a way to live healthier without sacrificing excellent-tasting food.

The possibilities are endless when choosing a specialization. It is important to remember that choosing a specialization does not limit you to working only for the clientele that is drawn to your particular specialization. However, choosing a niche can set you apart from other personal chefs and will draw in a clientele that is interested in the special services you can provide. Your specialty can also make you invaluable to your clients because you are providing them with foods that might be time consuming or difficult for them to prepare.

Who Hires Personal Chefs?

Every person who hires a personal chef is different. Many

either do not have the time to cook or simply do not enjoy cooking, so if they have the means to do so, they hire a personal chef to take the burden off them and save their time for other things.

Other clients might have dietary needs that make it difficult to cook flavorful food. These clients go to a personal chef because chefs have the expertise necessary to create foods within their dietary guidelines without sacrificing flavor.

The service you provide as a personal chef is very valuable and important to your customers. Many customers will be drawn to you because of your specialization or because they have heard about your work from other clients and want to try it for themselves.

What Education is Required to Become a Personal Chef?

Now that you know what a personal chef is and does, you are probably excited about starting your new career. However, you might have assumed that many years of specialized schooling are necessary to begin working as a chef. This chapter will give you information about the formalized education you might need before getting started and what to do if you do not have this education.

Do You Need a Formalized Education?

The idea of going through several years of culinary school, racking up thousands of dollars in student loans, and trying to balance school and a career can seem daunting. The good news is that you do not have to have a culinary background or meet any educational requirements to become a personal chef. You can start your business – and your new career – with your current talents and passion for cooking.

Of course, a culinary background and education does provide you with an advantage. If you already work as a chef in a restaurant or work in the food service industry, you might find your experience advantageous. Working in the industry helps to develop contacts and build a reputation for your services. People who are already familiar with you and the quality of your work will be more likely to hire you and provide you with referrals. These contacts and referrals can fuel your business.

Another advantage a culinary background or education is the opportunity to learn the trade and refine your cooking skills. In culinary school, you will have the chance to learn more about what foods complement each other, how to improve your dishes, how to effectively alter recipes to better suit your clients, and how to better time your cooking.

Culinary school and a culinary background will also provide you with a better understanding of cooking equipment and how it is used. This knowledge can help you learn how to save time and produce products more efficiently, which will give you the capacity to serve more clients.

If you are not already working in the culinary industry, do not be discouraged. You can still build your clientele, although it could potentially take more time. Many potential clients will want references and will ask about your background. Being able to provide references and showcase your experience will provide you with more credibility and will build a greater level of confidence in your abilities.

There are several ways to build credibility without a culinary background. One way is to offer your services to friends and family for parties, weddings, and banquets. Doing so will help establish you as a personal chef – it will prove that you are capable of doing the job and will get you in front of potential clients. Once a client has tasted and had a positive experience with your product, they will have a much higher level of confidence in your services and will be more likely to hire you.

Another way to establish yourself as a personal chef is to offer cooking classes in your community. A cooking class puts you in front of potential clients who will be able to see how you work and sample your food.

A third option to establish yourself as a personal chef is to find another personal chef in your area who has a full clientele and ask for an opportunity to work as an apprentice. This will help you learn the business from someone who already has a successful business and will help build your credibility.

What Are My Culinary Education Options?

An education in culinary arts is very hands on. The best way to learn to cook and refine your skills as a chef is practice often. You will have to constantly experiment and refine your cooking skills, even after you have completed your education.

Because of the hands-on nature of a career in culinary arts, a classroom environment is still the most popular and widely available option. Classroom learning puts you in the kitchen and gives you the freedom to experiment, receive critiques, and learn to improve.

Hands-on classroom learning will also help you learn more about the equipment you will be using and how to use it properly. You will learn how to cook a variety of foods to perfection and will get a chance to experiment with types of food you might have never worked with before, thereby building your expertise and ability to cater to the customer.

Some culinary arts schools even offer a personal chef specialization that will better prepare you for the challenges of running your own business and learning to cater to your clients needs.

Many major universities now offer a culinary arts program. There are also schools that specialize in just culinary-related fields. You can find a reputable culinary arts school in your area by asking others in the industry, using the Internet, looking in the yellow pages, or inquiring about course options in culinary arts with your local university.

If classroom learning is simply not an option for you due to family obligations, work, or proximity to a university, distance-learning options are available. In today's busy society, distance learning is becoming more readily available in most areas of study, offering you more options to choose from.

The best way to find a reputable distance learning program that will help you meet your needs is by checking with others in the industry. Choose a distance learning program that is going to give you the most comprehensive and thorough program possible. Talking to others in the culinary field who have used these distance learning programs can give you more insight into which distance learning programs will offer you the best education.

If you are brand new to the field and do not know anyone in the culinary industry, look for personal chefs in your area and see whether they would be willing to let you interview them. This will give you the opportunity to learn what education and background those who are successful in the field are obtaining and will give you a contact in the field.

Another way to find a distance learning program is to search the Internet. Be sure to read all the fine print and thoroughly check out the program offered before signing up or paying any money. You can also check with your state to see whether the program is accredited and recognized in your state.

It is important to do your research when choosing any program, especially a distance learning program. Although distance education and certification is becoming more readily available, it is still a buyer beware market.

If you start an apprenticeship with a chef who is already successful in the field, you might want to set up a cross-referral agreement with that chef. This will be especially helpful if you specialize in a specific type of cuisine. If your training chef has a full clientele, he or she may refer additional clients to your business. You can, in return, promise to offer them the same courtesy.

Although an education in culinary arts is not required to become a personal chef, having experience and education can help you build your business faster. Potential clients find chefs who have experience, education, and a proven track record to be more credible, capable, and better equipped to meet their personal needs.

The Culinary Business Academy

For many aspiring personal chefs, one of the best training programs is the Personal Chef Training program, available through the Culinary Business Academy. This program provides several options for you to obtain the training necessary to set up, start, and successfully operate your personal chef business, and avoid many of the mistakes typically made by new personal chefs.

Many new personal chefs opt for the Personal Chef Home Study Program offered by the Culinary Business Academy. This course includes the Professional Personal Chef Reference Manual, CDs that will assist you in learning to market and sell your services, and a collection of recipes that you can use as the core of your products. According to the Culinary Business Academy, this home study course can be completed in as little as two weeks; you can quickly prepare to begin your own personal chef venture. Upon completion of the course, you will have the option of taking three online tests – after successfully passing these tests, you will earn a diploma for the course and fulfill one of the requirements to become a Certified Personal Chef.

Some personal chefs find that they need training beyond that which is available through the home study course. The Culinary Business Academy also offers a 16-hour Quick Start Program, an intensive classroom training session taught by Certified Personal Chefs. This training session will give real world knowledge about the personal chef industry and allow you to get answers from people who have extensive experience providing personal chef services for clients. The Culinary Business Academy guarantees your success by refunding your tuition if you do not achieve a minimum level of business success after completing the Quick Start Program.

If a home study course is not for you, you can opt to obtain your diploma by taking the Personal Chef Undergraduate Program through the Culinary Business Academy, which is a five-day, onsite course that will give you accelerated training and help you get your personal chef business up and running quickly. The Culinary Business Academy also guarantees your success upon completion of this program.

For more information about the training programs offered by the Culinary Business Academy, visit their Web site at **www.culinarybusiness.com**.

Business Education and Experience

Although knowing and learning how to prepare meals that will turn your clients into long-term customers is essential to success as a personal chef, there are other types of knowledge you will need to keep your business profitable and turn your passion into a career.

An extensive understanding of business concepts will be very important. Taking business courses or pursuing a Master of Business Administration degree is one way to gain this business knowledge, but if you do not have the time or inclination to take college courses or pursue an advanced degree, there are other ways to gain the knowledge necessary to build and execute a successful business model.

One of the least expensive ways to gain all the business knowledge you will need to start and grow your business is to visit your local public library. The advantage you gain from visiting the library, other than saving thousands of dollars on books and tuition, is that you can learn practical applications as well as academic theory.

Here is a list of books that will help you understand how business works:

- *Legal Guide to Starting and Running a Small Business*, by Fred Steingold, ISBN 978-1413305135. This is an excellent book to help you decide how to form your business, make you aware of the legal considerations of running a business, and help you avoid some of the legal pitfalls that often plague business owners. It can also save you quite a bit of money in legal expenses, because you will not have to contact an attorney every time a legal question is raised. At over 450 pages, this book is no small undertaking, but if you can take the time to read it, you will have a thorough understanding of the legal considerations of being in business for yourself.

- *The Unofficial Guide to Starting a Business*, by Marcia Layton Turner, ISBN 978-0764572852. This thorough business guide demonstrates how to start a business from the very beginning stages to full operation. It also gives real-life examples that show practical applications of the concepts outlined in the book so you can see how the concepts will translate when you are building your personal chef business.

- *What No One Ever Tells You About Starting Your Own Business: Real Life Start Up Advice from 101 Successful Entrepreneurs*, by Jan Norman, ISBN 978-0793185962. Although this book is less concerned with providing a step-by-step guide to starting a business than other business books, it can be an excellent resource because it allows you to see the real-life successes and failures of entrepreneurs like you. You will get to see the mistakes that other business owners have made when starting and expanding their businesses and obtain tips from their successes.

- *The Complete Idiot's Guide to Starting Your Own Business*, 5th Edition, by Edward Paulson, ISBN 978-1592575848. This book provides all the information you need to launch your business with minimal difficulties. Edward Paulson breaks down business concepts into understandable terms and provides tips and insights along the way to give you every advantage possible while you are growing your personal chef business.

Regardless of whether you choose to pursue a formal business education, these books (and many others) can provide you with a strong foundation to bring your culinary skills to your community, while building a financially viable business that will support you and your family for many years to come.

Another way to gain insight into the world of business is to connect with other entrepreneurs in your area. You can obtain a wealth of knowledge about how to build a financially successful business by sitting down with people who have already built successful businesses and with people who are on the same path as you. This is an excellent way to get answers to questions you will have during your first few years as a professional personal chef.

You might be able to find local business owner groups via bulletin boards in local establishments, such as coffee shops, book stores, and other areas frequented by business owners. Do not be afraid to contact group organizers if you have questions about joining a group or attending meetings – the organizers will be happy to answer any questions you might have and help you feel comfortable with getting involved.

Business owner groups can also be excellent for networking. Once your business launches, you can provide other business owners with business cards or other promotional materials so they can pass these materials along to potential clients. Since they are probably busy building their own businesses, they might even elect to use your services themselves.

If you choose to promote your business through networking with other local business owners, be sure to offer to promote their businesses as well. This technique can work wonders for your business, especially if you are able to help your fellow business owners along the way.

Networking can also be a good way to learn where to obtain supplies at wholesale costs. If there are restaurant owners or other food service professionals in your group, they might be able to tell you where to obtain cooking equipment and ingredients at a discount, which can improve your profit margin. Other types of business professionals might help you save money on advertising materials, transportation, or other expenses you will incur as a result of doing business.

If there are several business owners who need similar types of materials or services, such as mailing, advertising, or insurance, you might be able to pool your financial resources with those of other business owners to obtain an even greater discount.

If you cannot find a business owners' group via a public bulletin board, you can try using **www.meetup.com** to find groups in your area. Signing up on this Web site is a quick and simple process, and you can find all available groups in your area within a matter of minutes. You will also find out when and where these groups meet and whether there are any membership dues or other costs to join and attend meetings.

If there are no available business owners' groups, you can start one on MeetUp. It is likely that there are other business owners in your area who could greatly benefit from attending meetings with other business owners, but have not taken the initiative to start a group. Starting a group on MeetUp costs $20, but this small fee can be well worth the benefits that you and the other business owners in your area will receive from networking and brainstorming sessions.

Now that you have learned about your education options, how to use any culinary experience you might have to your advantage, how to learn the business skills necessary to make your personal chef venture a success, and how to break into the personal chef business if you do not have education or experience to rely upon, let us move on to the first and most important step you will need to take to begin your career as a personal chef – creating and developing a business plan.

Developing a Business Plan

When you first considered starting a career as a personal chef, you might not have thought about the task of sitting down and detailing the background, vision, goals, and resources of your venture in a formalized document. However, you should formally detail all these elements in a business plan long before your first meal is ever served to a client. If you want to get your business off to a strong start and attract the support necessary to make your business a success, then a business plan is a vital first step.

Fortunately, creating a solid business plan is not nearly as difficult as it sounds, and there are plenty of resources available to help you write, organize, and present your business plan. This chapter will help you create your business plan, assist you in locating additional resources to help you refine your plan, and teach you how a good business plan can be valuable for you as a personal chef.

Why Do I Need a Business Plan?

When most people think of business plans, they think of a

document that is prepared for presentation to investors or loan officers in an attempt to raise capital for the opening or expansion of a business. While you might use your plan for these purposes at some point in your career as a personal chef, there are several reasons for creating a business plan that have nothing to do with obtaining financing or investment capital. These reasons are just as important to the ultimate success of your business, if not more so, than using a business plan for financial purposes.

Here are some of the most important uses for a business plan:

- *It forces you to research your business, your niche market, and the variables of the geographic area you will be serving.* Too often, people start a business with a great idea and very little else. A light bulb is a great idea, but not one that is going to do you much good if you fill your backpack with light bulbs to take on a journey through the rainforests of Guyana. Similarly, if you have a great idea for a personal chef business, you have to make sure that your business is appropriate for the people you want to serve.

  You have to make sure that your particular type of personal chef business is going to work with the types of customers living in the area you want to work in and convince yourself and others that similar businesses in demographically similar areas have already been successful. If you cannot convince yourself that your business will work, then you need to reevaluate your business strategy before you invest any additional time and money into your venture.

Writing a business plan is not about talking yourself out of starting your own business; it is about forcing yourself to objectively look at the realistic potential your business has for success in your geographic area.

- *It helps you identify potential obstacles to success in your business and determine feasible solutions that may be available.* Just as it is important to determine whether your personal chef business is appropriate for your area and the available clientele, it is also important to examine the potential obstacles to the success of your business and identify viable methods for dealing with those obstacles.

While optimism about your potential business success is usually good for motivating you and keeping you focused, your business plan is not the place to be optimistic. This is your opportunity to directly face the negative factors that could influence your finances and your business.

- *It helps keep you on track.* There will be times when you will lose focus or get so wrapped up in the minutia of running your personal chef business that you might forget the big picture – the objectives you had in mind when you started your career as a personal chef. Periodically reviewing your business plan can help you keep your focus and remind you of your goals.

Your business plan is not immutable; it will change as your business grows and changes, but it will always contain the same basic plan you devised when you started your career as a personal chef. This can be invaluable when you encounter the inevitable frustrations that come with working with the public and managing a business.

The Elements of a Business Plan

If you review a number of existing business plans, you will see that they reflect a wide range of styles; different types of businesses call for different plans, and a business plan for a manufacturing company will look very different than a business plan for a service business, such as yours. Although the section titles and styles may vary from plan to plan, all business plans contain the same basic elements.

Here are the elements that comprise all effective business plans. You can use these elements to craft a solid business plan that will convince your investors and lenders that you have thoroughly researched your business and help you plan your personal chef venture to handle all the challenges and opportunities that will come your way.

Executive Summary

The executive summary portion of your business plan will provide a quick overview of your business and introduce your readers to your venture. This section should be designed to make investors and lenders interested in your business, tell them about the background of your venture, and highlight any significant achievements of your business.

This section should be brief – you should be able to convey

all of the information in your executive summary in a half page to one page.

You should begin your executive summary with an overview of your business concept. Be specific but concise when describing your business. Writing "My business will provide meals to customers" is not a sufficient description of your business concept. Your investors will want to know what meals you will be providing, who your customers are, and why you stand to gain an advantage over other businesses providing similar services. "My business will provide healthy, low fat, ready-to-eat meals to working families in the Henderson area of Las Vegas, Nevada. Customers will be provided with complete nutritional information for each meal, which will appeal to families concerned about health and weight loss" is a much more detailed statement of a business concept and will help your readers understand that you are focused and are not trying to be all things to all people.

If you already have clients, you should provide current financial information about your personal chef business, including profits, sales figures, and the return you have received on your financial investments in the business.

You should also include information in your executive summary about your business' legal formation, the identity of the owner or owners of your business, the date your business was formed, and the identities of key personnel, if any.

If your business is already in operation, you should describe any major achievements of your business in a paragraph or two. If you have not yet commenced operations, you should describe any major achievements in your culinary career, such as promotions, educational milestones, or successful execution of catering services for a large event.

Finally, you will want to state the financial requirements of your business – in essence, the sum of money you are asking for from investors or lenders and the capital you will provide. You should also note any collateral you intend to use to secure loans, if you plan to show your business plan to lenders.

Again, it is very important that your executive summary be as brief as possible. Potential lenders and investors will want to be able to quickly understand the nature of your business, the background of the business, and the capital that will be required to start or expand the business. It is also important because a lengthy executive summary will give you the opportunity to include information that might suggest that your business is not well thought out or that you are undecided about the direction of your business.

Business Description

This section of your business plan will give readers a clear picture of the nature of your business. When you are writing this section, it is important to assume that your business plan readers have absolutely no knowledge of the personal chef business.

The first element of this section should tell your readers about the personal chef industry – what kinds of services personal chefs provide, what the present outlook is for people doing business as personal chefs, and any possible future developments within the industry that might create challenges or opportunities for your business. You should also describe the various markets that use personal chef services, as well as the competition seeking out the same clients as you.

When describing potential markets, general competition, and the present and future outlook for personal chefs, include your information sources in footnotes at the end of your business plan. Investors and lenders will want to see that you have thoroughly researched these topics. Guess work will not help you build a viable business, and it also will not convince lenders and investors to help you finance your business.

Another element of this section is the statement of the type of operation of your business and a brief reiteration of its legal form of ownership. You should also state whether your business is up and running yet.

For a personal chef, the type of operation will almost always be food service; however, if you will be teaching classes or packaging a portion of your products to be sold in local stores, the type of operation might cross over into service or manufacturing. It is permissible to state more than one type of operation, although you will want to carefully explain how the two operation types interconnect so that investors and lenders do not see your business as lacking focus.

Next, you will want to describe your target market, tell how you will distribute your products and administer services, and describe any support systems that will help your business succeed, such as advertising and marketing efforts, promotional offers, and support staff to handle schedule changes and meal requests for special occasions.

A very important element to include in the business description is a specific statement of how your business will gain and retain a competitive advantage. You can list specific competitors and tell how your business will provide service features that your competitors do not offer. Here are a few examples:

- Joe Smith's Personal Chef Service offers clients a choice of seven meal plans. In contrast, my service offers over two dozen meal plans and allows clients to modify each meal plan to add favorite dishes or delete meals that are not appealing to the clients' families.

- Jane Smith's Personal Chef Service allows clients to choose from a wide variety of meals based on the U.S.D.A. food pyramid. Similarly, my service offers meals based on the food pyramid, but also offers an array of choices for clients with specific dietary preferences, such as vegetarian and vegan meals, low carbohydrate dishes, and kosher meals.

- Jim Smith's Personal Chef Service offers clients meals that are prepared at an off-site business and delivers the refrigerated meals to clients' homes. My service gives clients the option to have the meals prepared in their homes so they can ensure that the preparation facilities are sanitary. This service will give clients peace of mind that Jim Smith's Personal Chef Service cannot.

• Judy Smith's Personal Chef Service offers entrees starting at $8.99 per person. My service will offer entrees starting at $6.99 per person for adults and will also offer smaller entrees for young children starting at $3.99 each.

These comparisons will demonstrate to readers that you have taken the time to evaluate the competition and to identify ways that you can offer something more to your clients.

Finally, your business description should demonstrate that you have researched the financial aspects of running a personal chef business and identified the strategies you will use to make your business profitable. Lenders and investors will want to see that you know not only how to keep your business running, but how to earn a profit with your business so that you can expand your operations and provide additional services to your clients.

The length of your business description will vary according to the complexity of your personal chef business, the types of products and services you offer to your clients, the number of relevant competitors in your service area, and the number of employees you will need to manage your client base and provide efficient, reliable service to your clients. As with your executive summary, you will want to be concise yet descriptive.

Market Strategies and Analysis

The third section of your business plan will delve into the specific markets you plan to attract with your services and how you plan to reach those markets.

You will want to begin this section by defining your market. "Families in Chicago" is very broad and will not allow you to gather the information necessary to develop a focus for your business. "Two income households in the Clarendon Hills area of Chicagoland" is much more useful for defining the marketing and service strategies of your personal chef venture.

When defining your market, you should include the size of that market (in terms of both geographical area and population), the family and living structure of the market, consumer trends within that market, and the opportunities for sales and profit the market offers.

The more narrowly you can define your target market, the more accurately you can forecast sales. For example, "two income households in the Clarendon Hills area of Chicagoland with children involved in extracurricular activities" is a very useful definition of your target market, because this market segment represents families that most likely have moderately high incomes and little time to spend on the preparation of meals.

The purpose of narrowly defining your market is to give you the information you need to correctly set pricing for your services and products, identify service strategies that will appeal to clients within that market, and develop marketing strategies to effectively reach people who are receptive to your services. Using the Clarendon Hills example above, you could use this definition to identify the number of other personal chefs serving that area, the prices charged by those chefs, the services that these competitors offer to clients, and the methods they use to promote their services. Once you have this information, you can begin identifying and developing your competitive advantages so that you can begin drawing business away from your competitors and tapping into market pockets that other personal chef services have overlooked.

Next, you will need to project the market share you believe your personal chef business will be able to gain within your target market. Although an accurate representation of potential market share can be difficult to determine and is a subjective figure, you can use data such as the size of your total target market, competitor pricing, the effectiveness of your marketing efforts, and the potential of your promotional offers to attract the interest of potential clients within your target market.

To arrive at a reasonable estimate of your total projected market share over the period of time your business plan covers, you will also need to conduct research that involves projecting total industry growth over that time period. Projecting your market share through anticipated industry growth requires the exploration of a number of different growth scenarios and determining how your business will respond to each of these scenarios.

Another method of anticipating your market share involves projecting the conversion rates of members of your target market that express interest in your services. To arrive at projected conversion rates, you should use historical industry conversion rates for personal chef services in your specific geographic area over a five-year cycle.

After you state your projected market share and the rationale used to arrive at that projection, you will need to tell your readers how you plan to develop your pricing for your products and services. A sophisticated plan for developing pricing is important because the prices you charge for your products and services will have a significant impact on the success of your business.

Many business owners believe that, in order to draw market share away from competition, they must consistently underprice their products and services. Although competitive pricing can be a useful element of your overall business promotion strategy, it is not essential that you always offer the cheapest services in the area. In fact, this can be detrimental to your business for two reasons:

- **First**, underpricing can erode the ability of your business to generate profits. Unless you can reduce the costs of materials, ingredients, advertising, transportation, and service, underpricing will leave your business with less money for payroll, equipment maintenance, and future growth. Without sufficient profit to sustain your business model, you can easily put yourself out of business by consistently undercutting your competition.

- **Second**, underpricing can give potential clients the impression that your products and services are inferior to those of other personal chefs serving the same area. Your meals might be just as good as, or even better than, the meals offered by your competition, but if you set your prices too low, you can create the impression that you give your clients less than they demand.

Arriving at a pricing structure for your products and services can be a complicated exercise. You want to offer clients excellent value for their money without appearing as though you are undercharging them. A thorough analysis of your costs and of the current pricing in the market as compared to the quality of the services offered by your competition will give you the basis for arriving at an optimal pricing structure.

After your complete the portion of your market strategies and analysis that outlines your chosen pricing structure, you should include a short subsection that identifies your product distribution channels. If your personal chef business operates on the simple business model of taking ingredients to a client's home, preparing the meals in the client's kitchen, and packaging the meals for refrigeration, the distribution analysis will be relatively brief and straightforward. If you use a more complicated business model that involves the cooperation of several junior chefs to assist with preparation and delivery, you might need to devote more space within your business plan to describing the distribution process.

The next element of the marketing analysis and strategies section should include an outline of your promotion plan for your personal chef business. Here, you will tell your readers how you plan to make members of your target market aware of your services and how you will convince them to hire you as a personal chef. You may identify the methods of advertising you will use, the introductory promotions you will offer, and the strategies you will employ to gain referrals from existing clients.

The final element of this section is an analysis of potential revenue from sales. In order to arrive at a projected revenue from your personal chef business, you will need to multiply the total projected market share you identified earlier in your market analysis and strategies section by the total dollar sales for each client over the period of time that the business plan covers. You can determine your total dollar sales per client by reviewing your pricing structure and estimating the number of meals or services that each client will purchase over the time period contemplated in the business plan.

Competitive Analysis

The competitive analysis section of your business plan will compare the position and business strategy of your personal chef business with the positions of your competitors. This will give your readers an idea of whether your business will be a viable competitor within your target market.

The first step in building a competitive analysis is to identify the competitors. You can either do this by simply identifying all the other personal chef services in your area that compete for the same clients or by identifying personal chef services in the same geographic area with similar competitive strategies. Although most people only consider businesses that compete for the same dollars, grouping businesses by competitive strategies can help you more accurately identify true competitors (personal chef services operating in your target market that have similar strategies and motivations) and incidental competitors (personal chef services operating in your target market that employ different strategies).

Once you have identified your business' true competitors, you can begin to analyze their business strategies to identify potential weaknesses that you can capitalize on. For example, suppose that Joe Smith's Personal Chef Service, like your own business, serves "two-income households in the Clarendon Hills area of Chicagoland with children involved in extracurricular activities." However, you notice that Joe Smith's Personal Chef Service only delivers meals to clients' homes on weekday afternoons.

Joe Smith is probably doing fine with his personal chef service because his clients have come to expect that he will deliver meals on weekday afternoons and will adjust their schedules to make sure someone is at the home to take delivery. You might wonder, however, how many people within your shared target market have not hired Joe Smith as a personal chef because they are unable or unwilling to arrange their schedules to accommodate Joe's delivery hours.

Joe Smith's limited delivery hours, coupled with the fact that he only delivers meals to clients' homes, might be a weakness in his business strategy. You might capitalize on this weakness by offering delivery hours until 7 p.m. or by offering delivery not only to clients' homes but to their workplaces as well. Both of these strategies serve to make using a personal chef service easier for clients and might attract a portion of your shared target market that Joe has inadvertently excluded in his business strategy.

When conducting a competitive analysis, you will want to make a list of your business' strengths and weaknesses in key business areas, such as the quality and variety of your products; the competitiveness of your pricing structure; the effectiveness, efficiency, and convenience of your product distribution methods; the ability of your promotional strategies to attract and retain clients, and the marketing strategies you will use to raise awareness of your products and services within your target market.

As in all sections of your business plan, it is crucial that you look at your business and the businesses owned by your competitors with a sense of objectivity and honesty. It will not do you or your lenders any good to trivialize your weaknesses or overstate the strengths of your business. In the long term, an inaccurate analysis of your competitive position can significantly impair your chances of success as a personal chef.

Business Development

The next section of your business plan is the business development section. In this part of your business plan, you will outline how your business will develop its products, its market, and its organization.

When describing development of your products, think about what products you will offer initially and what products you will introduce later in your personal chef career. For example, you might only provide a menu of 20 entrees in the beginning stages of your business but, as you expand your operations, you might plan to offer 50 entrees within a few years. You should describe how you will choose and develop your products and give your readers an idea of what objectives you plan to meet by offering additional products through your business.

Even if you are simply creating new meals to offer to your clients, product development will require financial resources. Your plan should detail how you will cover the costs of development, even if these costs are limited to purchasing additional cookware and ingredients to refine your new recipes at home.

To describe the development of your market, you will detail your promotions, your advertising strategies, and your plans for retaining clients and gaining client referrals. Like the product development subsection, your description of market development might reflect a plan with multiple phases, which you will implement as your business grows and you have more resources available.

If you do not plan to employ other people in your personal chef business, your description of your organizational development will be quite brief. If you plan to use staff members to handle some of the business functions, though, you will want to describe the hierarchy of your business and note how your business will generate sufficient revenue to cover payroll expenses.

The final part of this section addresses risks associated with developing your products, your market, and your organization. Each type of development carries inherent risks – for example, when you develop a new meal to add to your personal chef menu, you incur several distinct risks:

- Your new meal could be ill received and cause you to lose clients who opt to try it.

- Your meal could contain ingredients that trigger allergic reactions for certain clients.

- Your meal could be very similar to one already offered by a competitor, which could cause a legal dispute.

- Freezing or refrigeration might substantially reduce the quality and flavor of your meal.

When addressing the risks associated with the development of your business, you should document how you will handle these risks. Your business plan should show your readers how you will minimize each risk and how you will deal with the effects of these risks if they occur.

Operations and Management Plan

The "Operations and Management Plan" section of your business plan will address your organizational and operations structure. Essentially, this section will give your readers a picture of how your business functions on a day-to-day basis.

Your operations and management plan will detail what management and staff positions exist within your business and what tasks each team member is responsible for.

Of course, if you work by yourself and never plan to expand your business to the point where you require support staff and management to continue your operations, this section will be brief. However, if you do anticipate expanding your business, it is very likely that you will need to hire talented professionals to assume various roles within your business. Your business plan will help you streamline the functions of each position so that you can create an efficient business that does not place a disproportionate share of responsibility on any one individual.

If you do not yet know how many staff members you will need to effectively manage your business and carry out its functions, a good way to determine this is to look at the tasks themselves. First, you will need to define the tasks your business will need to carry out to operate efficiently and profitably.

Defining tasks in this section requires a broad focus, rather than a detailed, narrow one. For example, some of the broad tasks that might be requirements of a personal chef business are:

- Marketing

- Promotion development and implementation

- Procurement of supplies and ingredients for meals

- Preparation of meals

- Transportation of supplies, ingredients, or finished meals

- Administrative functions, such as customer service, payroll, and coordination of employee benefits

- Accounting

- Banquet or special event coordination

After you have broadly defined the tasks required to operate your personal chef business, you will need to identify the types of personnel you will need to handle each of these tasks and determine the number of each type of professional you will need to meet the goals of your business. Then, conduct research to determine the prevailing wages for each type of professional. You can use a Web site, such as **www.salary. com**, to help you determine wages for different types of professionals in your area. This will help you determine your overall expenses for payroll.

Once you have determined and stated your payroll expenses in your business plan, you will need to calculate your overhead expenses. This includes expenses for items such as transportation, advertising and promotion, equipment, product packaging, unrecoverable fees for services provided to your clients, liability and property damage insurance, and loan payments.

Your payroll and overhead expense calculations will allow you to determine and state your capital requirements for starting, operating, and expanding your business. Your capital requirements calculation represents the total amount of money necessary to keep your business running. With most businesses, a portion of the capital requirements will come from investments and loans and the remainder from capital provided by the business owner or owners.

The final element of this section is a calculation of the cost of goods – that is, the amount that each sale will cost you, in terms of the sum of materials used (such as ingredients), the payroll expenses for the employees required to operate and manage your business, and the overhead costs that you will incur as a function of operating your personal chef service.

Determining the cost of goods is easier for a personal chef business than for retail or wholesale businesses. This is because many types of retail and wholesale businesses must consider not only the costs of goods that are already sold, but also the costs of goods that remain in inventory. A personal chef business will most likely not have meals that remain in inventory, because you will purchase ingredients and prepare meals based on orders made by your clients.

Financial Components

The final section of your business plan is the financial components section, which contains a series of three statements that your investors and lenders will want to see: the income statement, the cash flow statement, and the balance sheet.

The income statement gives your investors, lenders, and other readers a clear picture of the ability of your business to generate cash. It should be stated on a monthly basis for the first year, a quarterly basis for the second year, and a yearly basis for subsequent years.

Your income statement will include the following elements:

- **Income:** All income generated by your personal chef business, from all sources.

- **Cost of goods:** Costs associated with the sale of products in inventory. Since you will not likely keep meals in inventory, your income statement will reflect a low cost of goods.

- **Gross profit margin:** The difference between income and cost of goods. You can either express the gross profit margin as a dollar amount or a percentage.

- **Operating expenses:** All labor and overhead expenses associated with running your business.

- **Total expenses:** The sum of all labor and overhead expenses listed in operating expenses above.

- **Net profit:** The difference between gross profit margin and total expenses.

- **Depreciation:** The reduction in value of assets, such as cooking equipment and vehicles used to generate income.

- **Net profit before interest:** Net profit less depreciation.

- **Interest:** All interest derived from short-term and long-term loans.

- **Net profit before taxes:** The difference between net profit before interest and interest.

- **Taxes:** All taxes incurred as a result of operating your personal chef business.

- **Profit after taxes:** The difference between net profit

before taxes and the taxes incurred as a result of your business operations.

- **Summary:** A brief synopsis of your income statement that analyzes the income potential of your business and highlights any key points that will be of interest to your investors and lenders.

The cash flow statement shows how much cash your business will require to meet its financial obligations. It also shows when that cash will be available to you, and where it will come from. Based on the costs incurred and the cash available to meet those costs, your business will either show a profit or a loss at the end of each month. This is important because if your projections show a loss, it is an indication that you have not accounted for everything.

When drafting your cash flow statement, it is important that you prepare your statement on a monthly basis for the first year of operations, then on a quarterly basis for the second year. This is because you will incur the majority of your expenses for equipment and other nonrecurring expenses during the first two years, and much of your revenue during this period will go toward purchasing additional supplies to build your business and make sure that you are able to meet increasing customer demand for your services.

Here are the items you will need to include in your cash flow statement:

- **Cash sales:** All sales derived from your business operations that are paid to you in cash.

- **Receivables:** All income derived from sales that are paid to you in a form other than cash.

- **Other income:** All income that is derived from sources other than sales of your personal chef services, such as investments, liquidated assets, and interest on loans that you have extended to others.

- **Total income:** The total of cash sales, receivables, and other income.

- **Materials:** The costs of ingredients used to prepare the meals you sell to your clients and supplies purchased to create these meals.

- **Production:** The cost of labor required to prepare, package, transport, and deliver meals to clients.

- **Overhead:** The sum of all fixed and variable expenses required to operate your business.

- **Marketing and advertising:** All costs associated with marketing and promoting your business, including salaries of any marketing personnel.

- **Research and development:** Costs associated with researching customer needs and developing products to offer to your clients.

- **Administration:** All costs incurred for providing administrative functions of your business, such as payroll and employee benefits.

- **Taxes:** All taxes incurred as a result of your business operations, except for payroll taxes.

- **Capital requirements:** Any capital needed to purchase equipment and generate additional income.

- **Loan payments:** The costs of making installment payments on loans you have taken out to start or build your business.

- **Total expenses:** The total amount of expenses your business will incur as a result of operating your personal chef business.

- **Cash flow:** The difference between your total income and your total expenses. You will also list this amount as beginning cash for the next period.

- **Cumulative cash flow:** The difference between the cash flow for the current period and the cash flow from the previous period.

- **Summary:** A short synopsis of your cash flow statement that highlights key points and analyzes the overall cash flow statement.

Your balance sheet will use information derived from the financial section to develop an overall picture of your business' finances on an annual basis. The balance sheet will contain summarized information broken down into assets, liabilities, and equity.

Your assets will include cash available from the previous period, accounts receivable, inventory, and total current assets (the sum of cash, accounts receivable, supplies, and inventory). It will also include long-term assets, such as investments, equipment, and real estate. Any calculations for equipment and owned real estate will factor in depreciation of the property.

Liabilities include accounts payable, accrued liabilities such as overhead and payroll, and taxes. It also includes long-term liabilities such as mortgage and loan payments.

Equity is simply the difference between assets and liabilities. The equity that you own in your business is one of the key determining factors that investors and lenders use to calculate the amount of capital they are willing to contribute to your business.

Now that you have learned the elements of a business plan and how they are used to build a blueprint for your business and attract capital from investors and lenders, it might be helpful for you to see a sample business plan tailored to a personal chef business so you can see how these elements look in a practical application.

The following pages contain a sample business plan that incorporates all the elements outlined in this chapter.

BUSINESS PLAN: DINNER IN A FLASH, LLC

I. Executive Summary

Introduction

Dinner in a Flash is a mobile personal chef service serving busy families in Westerville, Ohio, an upscale suburb of Columbus that is primarily populated by two-income households. Dinner in a Flash intends to capture the interest of Westerville families by providing ready-to-eat meals that are healthy, made with premium ingredients, and derived from a variety of regional cuisines. The company expects to quickly build a strong business presence in the Westerville area, due to the industry experience of the company owners and the limited competition operating in this area.

BUSINESS PLAN: DINNER IN A FLASH, LLC

Dinner in a Flash intends to offer high quality meals at competitive prices to meet the needs of middle- to high-income families living and working in the Westerville area.

The Company

Dinner in a Flash is a limited liability company licensed in the state of Ohio. It is equally owned and managed by the company's two partners, Joe and Jan Smith.

Mr. Joe Smith has over ten years experience in the food service industry, having worked as the head chef of Estrella Restaurante, an upscale Mexican restaurant in Columbus, Ohio, and La Italia, an exclusive Italian restaurant in Philadelphia. Mrs. Jan Smith has also worked in the food service industry for over a decade, having held the position of Marketing Director for Le Boehme, a full service restaurant and catering business in Columbus' German Village area.

The company intends to hire a sous chef, a full-time delivery driver, and a promotions director to attract new clients and provide meal preparation support for the company's day-to-day operations.

Products and Services

The company plans to initially offer 40 meals that derive influences from cuisines, such as traditional American, Italian, Mexican, South Indian, and Japanese. The company will cater to its clients by devising meal plans tailored to each client's personal preferences, dietary needs, and religious food restrictions.

Dinner in a Flash will give clients the option of having fully prepared meals delivered to their home or office or having the meals prepared in the clients' own kitchens.

The company will focus on using fresh, healthy ingredients, limiting use of oils and fats during preparation, and minimizing use of freezing to ensure that clients receive high quality, nutritious, and delicious meals to encourage client retention and referrals.

BUSINESS PLAN: DINNER IN A FLASH, LLC

The Market

The demand for personal chef services has increased exponentially over the past decade, both nationally and in the Columbus, Ohio area. The rise in two-income households with children, coupled with an increased consumer focus on dietary health, stimulates consumer demand for quick, nutritious meals that can easily be heated and served within the constraints of clients' busy schedules.

Dinner in a Flash intends to establish a large repeat client base and will concentrate its marketing efforts in the Westerville area to attract long-term clients. In addition to Westerville area residents, Dinner in a Flash expects to derive approximately 15 percent of its sales from business travelers staying in Westerville's many hotels and business suites. High-visibility marketing and attractive promotions are essential to capturing the interest of the company's target market.

Financial Considerations

Dinner in a Flash intends to raise $75,000 of its own capital and borrow $75,000 in the form of an SBA approved loan. This provides all the financing required to start the business and complete its first year in business.

Dinner in a Flash should break even by the sixth month of its operations as sales and long-term clients steadily increase. The company anticipates sales of $140,000 the first year, $220,000 the second year, and $300,000 the third year of operations. Profits for this period are expected to be $17,000 for the first year, $25,000 for the second year, and $45,000 for the third year.

II. Business Description

Industry Summary

The personal chef industry provides meals that are easy to heat and serve for busy working adults, senior citizens, and other people who lack the time

BUSINESS PLAN: DINNER IN A FLASH, LLC

or ability to prepare healthy, delicious meals. Personal chefs deliver already prepared meals to clients' homes or offices or travel to clients' homes to prepare the meals.

Presently, the personal chef industry is enjoying a significant increase in demand, fueled by the growing number of two-income households with children to care for and by the increase of senior citizens that choose to live independently.

The primary challenge faced by personal chefs is serving multiple clients during the same working hours. Because clients typically request meals for dinner rather than lunch or breakfast, the necessary peak delivery hours for personal chefs is between 5:30 p.m. and 7:30 p.m. on weekdays.

Little competition exists locally for personal chefs serving the Westerville area. At present, there are only two personal chefs targeting Westerville's 60,000 residents. Roger Hammerstein's Personal Chef Service offers preparation of meals in clients' homes, but does not offer office delivery of meals. Gilbert Sullivan's Personal Chef Service offers both home and office delivery of meals, but offers only traditional American cuisine with minimal emphasis on low fat ingredients. Dinner in a Flash intends to offer low fat meals, varied cuisines, and both home and office delivery to capture a majority of the market share in this area.

Company Summary

Dinner in a Flash is a personal chef service owned and managed by two partners. It is primarily engaged in the food service business. These partners represent the food preparation and delivery functions and the sales and marketing functions, respectively. The partners will provide funding from their own savings and investments, which will cover start-up expenses and provide a financial cushion for the first year of business operations. A ten-year SBA loan will provide the remainder of the capital for the first year of operations. The owners expect to build a strong presence in the Westerville area, due to the owner's experience in the food service industry and the low level of competition in the area.

BUSINESS PLAN: DINNER IN A FLASH, LLC

The company's target market is two-income households in the Westerville area. The company will focus its marketing efforts on middle- to upper-income families, and plans to reach its target market through the distribution of flyers, local online message board banners, a dedicated Web site, and community newspaper advertisements. After the initial startup, Dinner in a Flash expects to receive referral clients by providing discounts to existing clients in exchange for the referrals.

Company Ownership

Dinner in a Flash is licensed as a limited liability company in the state of Ohio and is equally owned by its two partners, Joe and Jan Smith.

Company History

Dinner in a Flash is a startup company, which will be financed by the owners' own capital and a ten-year SBA loan.

Products

Dinner in a Flash will prepare and deliver ready-to-heat meals from a variety of regional cuisines. The ingredients in 34 of the 40 meals available can be adapted to meet dietary restrictions, such as kosher, vegetarian, and vegan diets.

The meals are delivered for refrigeration at the clients' homes and offices in disposable foil containers with vented plastic lids to allow for easy microwave preparation.

III. Marketing Strategies and Analysis

Target Market

Dinner in a Flash has established middle- to high-income, two-income households living and working in the Westerville area as its target market.

BUSINESS PLAN: DINNER IN A FLASH, LLC

The geographic area of this target market, Westerville, Ohio, consists of approximately 40 square miles occupying the northeast section of Columbus, a city with a metropolitan area of approximately 1.5 million residents. Of Westerville's 60,000 residents, approximately 16,000 residents comprise the target market sought by the company.

Historically, the target market has relied heavily on fast food and casual restaurants to provide meals between work and family activities. Members of the target market often have difficulty finding time to plan meals, visit a grocer, or prepare and serve meals. Dinner in a Flash plans to offer a healthy alternative to fast food and casual restaurant meals that are often high in fat and low in nutrients.

Over a three-year period, Dinner in a Flash intends to capture 30 percent of the target market. Although meals provided by the other two personal chef services in the area, Roger Hammerstein's Personal Chef Service and Gilbert Sullivan's Personal Chef Service, are sold at prices nearly identical to those that will be sold by Dinner in a Flash, the company intends to capture market share by providing healthy, fresh meals that can be delivered to either the home or office.

The company also intends to capture market share through extensive use of its client referral program, which provides significant discounts to existing clients for referring friends, family, and business associates to the company.

The projected market share over a three-year period is supported by nationwide industry information, which shows that personal chef services in similar demographic areas with less than five competing services are able to capture 20 to 40 percent of the available market share by using marketing techniques similar to those contemplated by Dinner in a Flash.

Product Pricing

The company has established pricing by analyzing the pricing structures of personal chef services operating in the Columbus metropolitan area and

BUSINESS PLAN: DINNER IN A FLASH, LLC

personal chef services operating in metropolitan areas of similar size. Entrees will sell for prices between $7.99 and $11.99, and full meals will sell for prices between $9.99 and $14.99. These prices are similar to those charged by Roger Hammerstein's Personal Chef Service and Gilbert Sullivan's Personal Chef Service.

Distribution

The company's business model provides two primary channels of distribution. First, the meals may be prepared in Dinner in a Flash's production facility in Westerville, Ohio, and transported to clients' homes and offices for refrigeration. Second, the clients may elect to have the ingredients transported to their homes so that the meals can be prepared in their own kitchens. The first distribution method allows for ease of delivery and minimizes the time the clients need to spend at home to obtain the meals; the second distribution method gives clients the peace of mind of knowing where the food is being prepared, so they can have direct control over the condition of the preparation facility.

For the first six months, all meal deliveries will be handled by Joe Smith. After that period, Dinner in a Flash intends to hire a full-time delivery driver to distribute approximately 75 percent of the meals not being prepared in the clients' own homes, which will allow the company to take on more clients and significantly expand sales.

Competitive Analysis

There are two personal chef services currently serving the Westerville area: Roger Hammerstein's Personal Chef Service and Gilbert Sullivan's Personal Chef Service. Both companies advertise and cater to the same target market as Dinner in a Flash.

Price point will not be a primary consideration for gaining market share. The prices charged by Dinner in a Flash will be comparable to those charged by the other personal chef services in the Westerville area. Instead, Dinner in a Flash intends to focus on benefits not offered by competing services.

The company intends to compete with Roger Hammerstein's Personal Chef Service by offering a distribution model not offered by that competitor: delivery

BUSINESS PLAN: DINNER IN A FLASH, LLC

of ready made meals to both homes and workplaces in the Westerville area. This will gain interest from clients who need personal chef services, but are not comfortable with allowing a personal chef to spend several hours each week in their homes.

The company intends to compete with Gilbert Sullivan's Personal Chef Service by focusing on providing meals from varied regional cuisines and using fresh, low fat ingredients that will be attractive to clients focused on weight loss and improved dietary health.

The company's primary challenge in competing with the existing personal chef services in the Westerville area will be initial name recognition. Both services have been doing business in the Westerville area for approximately five years and have built a significant presence in the community. Dinner in a Flash intends to gain market visibility by utilizing targeted, aggressive advertising; implementing promotions to gain referrals; and sponsoring community activities, such as Westerville's little league baseball team.

IV. Business Development

Strategy and Implementation

Dinner in a Flash will succeed by providing healthy, low fat meals to suit a variety of tastes and preferences and by offering delivery of ready-to-heat meals to both homes and offices in the Westerville area.

Competitive Edge

The company's competitive edge lies in the low level of competition doing business in the Westerville area and the enhanced services offered to clients.

Sales Strategy

As the chart below indicates, Dinner in a Flash anticipates sales of $140,000 in its first year of operations, $220,000 in its second year, and $300,000 in its third year.

BUSINESS PLAN: DINNER IN A FLASH, LLC			
Unit Sales	2008	2009	2010
Ready Made Meals	$94,000	$168,000	$240,000
Meals Prepared in Clients' Homes	$46,000	$52,000	$60,000
Total Unit Sales	$140,000	$220,000	$300,000
Direct Cost of Sales	2008	2009	2010
Ready Made Meals	$85,000	$149,500	$204,000
Meals Prepared in Clients' Homes	$38,000	$41,000	$51,000
Total Direct Cost of Sales	$123,000	$190,500	$255,000

Product Development

Initially, Dinner in a Flash will offer approximately 40 meals that clients can choose from. These meals will reflect a number of regional cuisines, and most can be altered to suit a particular client's dietary needs or personal preferences.

The company plans to develop an additional ten meals during its first year of operations. The selection of these meals will be based on responses on comment cards distributed to existing clients. The owners' contributed capital, along with capital derived from a ten-year SBA loan, will cover the cost of purchasing additional cookware and developing the new meals.

Organizational Structure

The two owners will equally own Dinner in a Flash. Initially, the two owners will also be the sole employees of the company. After six months of operations, the company intends to hire a full-time delivery driver, a promotions director, and a sous chef to facilitate expansion of the business.

The sous chef and promotions director will be paid a yearly salary, and the

BUSINESS PLAN: DINNER IN A FLASH, LLC

delivery driver will be paid a flat fee per delivery. In addition, all employees will be paid a profit-sharing bonus each March, based on profit for the preceding year.

Business Development Risks

The primary risks associated with the planned operations of the company are personal and professional liability and reduction of the final quality of meals delivered to clients' homes and offices due to freezing or refrigeration time.

Dinner in a Flash will address the risks associated with personal and professional liability to clients by purchasing a business liability policy with a low deductible and a liability limit of $2,000,000. In addition, it will purchase business automobile insurance with liability limits of $100,000 per person and $300,000 per accident to cover incidents occurring during delivery of the meals.

The company plans to address the potential reduction of meal quality through refrigeration and freezing by conducting extensive testing before any marketing efforts begin. The use of fresh ingredients and minimal use of oils will minimize any reduction in quality that might occur due to refrigeration. Also, meal plans will be designed with refrigeration time in mind, so that meals that can withstand freezing or longer refrigeration times will be scheduled at the end of the clients' weekly purchasing cycle.

V. Operations and Management Plan

Dinner in a Flash intends to remain a small company, requiring few employees to carry out the company's day-to-day operations.

Initially, Joe Smith will serve as the company's sole chef and delivery person. Jan Smith will serve as the company's advertising and promotions director while handling administrative functions, such as client calls and accounting.

Dinner in a Flash anticipates that, after six months of operation, sales will

BUSINESS PLAN: DINNER IN A FLASH, LLC

require the company to add additional staff. At that time, the company intends to hire professionals for the following positions:

- Sous chef: This person will be responsible for the preparation of soups and stews included in the meals. This person might also handle some of the other meal preparations as necessary to keep pace with consumer demand.

- Promotions director: This person will be responsible for developing and implementing promotions to attract new clients and to retain existing clientele. This includes implementation of discounts and incentives, as well as sponsoring community events that will help the company gain visibility in the Westerville area.

- Delivery driver: This person will be responsible for delivering meals prepared at the company's production facility to the homes and offices of clients. Expected delivery hours will be from 11 a.m. to 6:30 p.m. on weekdays and from 8 a.m. to 12 p.m. on Saturdays.

Payroll Expenses

Dinner in a Flash anticipates that the addition of these three positions will increase payroll expenses by $85,000 annually; however, the projected sales increases will support the addition of these employees.

Overhead Expenses

Dinner in a Flash expects to incur the majority of its overhead expenses at startup. The production facility is wholly owned by Joe and Jan Smith, with no mortgage or other loan on the property.

The capital required for purchasing cookware, a delivery van, and other startup equipment will be derived from the owners' contributed capital and a ten-year SBA loan. The company expects to incur startup overhead expenses of approximately $120,000.

BUSINESS PLAN: DINNER IN A FLASH, LLC

Additional expenses, such as those for packaging, ingredients, and vehicle maintenance, will be realized over the life of the business. Dinner in a Flash uses a unique business model under which products are sold and paid for before they are produced. This puts the company in the unique position of having no significant storage or inventory expenses.

Cost of Goods

Dinner in a Flash has negotiated contracts with several wholesalers to purchase the majority of the ingredients used in meal preparation directly. The company expects the cost of producing each meal to be between $4 and $7, with an overall first year cost of goods of approximately $123,000, which includes approximately $52,000 for ingredients and $71,000 for advertising, promotion, overhead expenses, and employee salaries.

VI. Financial Components

INCOME STATEMENT

	Jan 08	Feb 08	Mar 08	Apr 08	May 08	Jun 08
Income	$5,000	$5,500	$7,000	$7,500	$7,500	$8,000
Cost of Goods	$4,500	$4,700	$5,200	$5,500	$5,500	$5,800
Gross Profit Margin	$700	$750	$800	$850	$850	$900
Operating Expenses	$4,500	$4,700	$5,200	$5,500	$5,500	$5,800
Total Expenses	$4,500	$4,700	$5,200	$5,500	$5,500	$5,800
Net Profit	$700	$750	$800	$850	$850	$900
Depreciation	$100	$100	$100	$100	$100	$100
Net Profit Before Interest	$600	$650	$700	$750	$750	$800
Interest	$100	$100	$100	$100	$100	$100
Net Profit Before Taxes	$500	$550	$600	$650	$650	$700

BUSINESS PLAN: DINNER IN A FLASH, LLC

INCOME STATEMENT

Taxes	$200	$200	$200	$200	$200	$200
Profit after Taxes	$300	$350	$400	$450	$450	$500

CASH FLOW STATEMENT

	Jan 08	Feb 08	Mar 08	Apr 08	May 08	Jun 08	
Cash Sales	$5,000	$5,500	$7,000	$7,500	$7,500	$8,000
Receivables	$0	$0	$0	$0	$0	$0
Other Income	$0	$0	$0	$0	$0	$0
Total Income	$5,000	$5,500	$7,000	$7,500	$7,500	$8,000
Materials	$2,000	$2,200	$4,500	$4,700	$4,700	$5,000
Production	$200	$220	$450	$4,700	$470	$500
Overhead	$2,000	$2,200	$2,200	$2,200	$2,200	$2,200
Marketing	$500	$500	$500	$500	$500	$500
Research and Development	$0	$0	$0	$100	$100	$100
Administration	$300	$300	$300	$300	$300	$300
Taxes	$200	$200	$200	$200	$200	$200
Capital Requirements	$6,000	$6,500	$6,700	$7,000	$7,500	$8,000
Loan Payments	$400	$400	$400	$400	$400	$400
Total Expenses	$4,500	$4,700	$5,200	$5,500	$5,500	$5,800
Cash Flow	$300	$350	$400	$450	$450	$500
Cumulative Cash Flow	$300	$650	$1,050	$1,500	$1,950	$2,450

BALANCE SHEET

Assets: $140,000

Liabilities: $123,000

Equity: $17,000

4

Setting Up a Business Budget

Although setting up a budget can seem daunting for the new business owner, it is a necessary step to starting and running a successful business. A budget can keep you from having to cut corners in certain areas of your business' finances and can mean the difference between a successful, profitable operation and a failed business venture.

Regardless of the type of business you are starting, you will need money to get the business off the ground. In order to get clients, you will have to budget for the necessary supplies and the cost of marketing to potential clients. These can be costly investments, especially when you are trying to get your business off the ground. A well planned budget can also help you to start seeing a profit earlier and allow you to take on more clients quicker than if you did not take the time to draft a budget.

If you are the primary bread winner for your family or you are single and living on your income alone, it will be very difficult for you to immediately quit your day job. With any business, it takes several months, sometimes even several years, to start making a profit. You will still need to pay your bills and be able to support yourself while starting up your business, in addition to building capital for the startup costs of your personal chef service, such as equipment, advertising, and purchase of ingredients and packaging. It is recommended that you save up at least six months of your current income before you start relying on your business for your primary income.

It might seem impossible to save up one half of your yearly salary, especially if you are unhappy in your current job, but it can be done. The first step is to cut as much of your monthly spending as possible. Look at what you are currently bringing in each month as opposed to what you are spending. Then, determine what bills or expenses can be cut. For example, if you never watch television but are paying for cable services, consider shutting off your cable – this represents an unnecessary expense that can help you save hundreds of dollars over the course of a year. If you spend a significant amount of money eating out, find ways to cut back on dining – your meal expenses can double as research expenses if you serve your family the meals that you are developing for your personal chef business. If you are spending an exorbitant amount on groceries, try clipping coupons or using less expensive store brands. These may seem like small changes, but any cuts you can make in your monthly budget can help you save up for your business goals – freedom from working for someone else and the ability to be your own boss.

Although it can take up a significant amount of time that you would rather be devoting to your business, another way to secure enough income to start your business is to moonlight. Start building a clientele and take on as many clients as you can before quitting your day job. You will be busy and will not have as much time to devote to yourself or your family, but it will not be forever. You will be building your business and will have something to start from when you are able to leave your current job.

You can also talk to family and friends about investing in your company. They will, in turn, receive a return on their investment as your business becomes more profitable. This can help you get started faster, but any investor in your company will share in your profit, making your own take-home pay less than it would be if you were not splitting the profits.

You can also find other personal chefs to go into business with. You and the other chef can invest and pool your income for start-up costs. Your company would be able to take in more clientele because the work load would be shared by more than one chef. You could then divide profit based on the number of clients that each chef brings in.

Another option, although not recommended, is to cash in investment accounts such as 401(k)s. It is important to remember before choosing this option that you will be charged a penalty fee and taxes – you will be losing a percentage of your investment in the end. It is also important to remember that you will lose the retirement investment you have taken so long to build.

You might also want to look into a small business loan to start up your business. There are a variety of small business loans available to help you get your business up and running. You will want to spend some time on your budget before applying for the loan so that you can determine how much you will need to get started. Take time to shop for your small business loan so that you can find the best possible rate. The interest rates of loans will vary based on the length of the loan.

Another important step in building a business budget is to determine start-up cost. Many new business owners underestimate the amount of money it will take to start their businesses. To determine start-up cost, make a list of all the supplies you will need to prepare the food for your clients. Then, identify the cooking items from that list you already have. Although you might need to add some things, you probably already own some of the items you will need and might be able to use them in the early stages of your business.

If you have decided to rent a kitchen space, you will need to start shopping for your location to get a realistic idea about how much it will cost to lease a space. First, you will need to get an idea of how much room you will need. Next, you will have to determine what equipment you will need to completely stock your kitchen. Will you be able to lease any of the equipment, or will you have to purchase it all?

If you will be transporting food, you will need to factor in the cost of purchasing a vehicle and converting it to meet your specific business needs. You will also have to set up a home office. Your office will be used for client files, your computer, and printer. You might also need to invest in a fax machine and copier. Office supply stores normally have a selection of machines that will serve as both a fax and a copier. You might even need to have a separate business phone line installed.

As a business owner, you will also be responsible for creating invoices and keeping track of business expenses. You might want to look into purchasing accounting software to keep track of your business expenses.

Another option for tracking your business expenses is to hire an accountant. An accountant can be a valuable resource for helping you keep track of your business expenses and taxes. If you choose to hire an accountant, you will need to factor the accountant's fees into your budget.

You will need to set aside a realistic budget for marketing. No matter how good of a chef you are or how well-stocked your kitchen is, your business will not go anywhere without clients. Marketing is critical to reaching your potential clients and getting them interested in hiring you. Your marketing will get you in front of your potential clients so you can show them how their services will meet their needs. It is important to be realistic about your marketing expenses. You will need to set up a marketing plan and begin researching the cost for your chosen marketing methods. You will learn how to build a detailed marketing plan in a later chapter of this book.

If you plan to hire employees, payroll will be another expense to figure into your budget. For many larger companies, payroll is the largest expense in the budget. You might eventually need to provide employee benefits, such as health insurance.

You will also be doing plenty of traveling. If you choose to cook in your clients' kitchens, you will have to figure in the cost of gas for traveling to and from the clients' homes. You will also have to consider the transportation costs of making trips to the store to shop for your clients' food.

If you are cooking in your own kitchen or are renting a space, you will still have the cost of transporting entrees to and from your clients' homes and transportation to and from the store.

As you can see, some of these elements will be ongoing in your budget, while others will be one time start-up costs or incidental costs, such as the replacement of equipment. Marketing and transportation will be ongoing expenses in your budget.

Once you have identified the items that will be necessary to include in your budget, determine the source of your start-up income. Once you have determined how much start-up money you have, you can begin to determine how much money to allot to each part of your budget.

Not all parts of your budget will need to be assigned equal amounts of your money. For example, you might have most of the cooking equipment you need, but you have identified a few items you will need to add. This portion of your budget will not need to be allotted as much money as your marketing plan.

Your system for mapping your budget can be as simple or elaborate as you wish. You can write down each itemized area on your budget and write the maximum amount that can be spent for each section, or you may choose to purchase software to help you track the items on your budget.

It might be wise to add a miscellaneous section to your budget in case you go over budget on some of your items or other unforeseen circumstances arise.

5

What Equipment Does a Personal Chef Need?

Whether you are cooking in a rented kitchen, your own kitchen, or your client's kitchen, there is a significant amount of equipment you will need to have on hand. As a personal chef, you must always be prepared by having the proper equipment necessary to prepare the meals that will attract long-term clients and generate a long list of referrals.

If they will be preparing meals in the kitchens of clients, most personal chefs take everything they need with them to a client's home. Your portable kitchen must be well-equipped and easy to transport. It is critical that you keep your equipment organized so you can find everything with ease when you are in your client's kitchen. It is also important that everything is clean and sanitary.

Here is a list of some of the basic cooking items and utensils you will want to include in your portable kitchen:

- Pressure Cooker

- Two 12-inch nonstick skillets

- Multiple cooking racks

- Vacuum Sealer

- At least one 12-inch lid to use on your 12-inch skillets

- One four-quart saucepan with a lid

- One cast-iron grill pan

- One Dutch oven with a lid

- At least two plastic cutting boards

- Disposable cutting mats to use with your cutting boards

- Stainless-steel or plastic mixing bowls

- Plastic colander

- Fine mesh strainer

- Four nonstick baking sheets with sides

- Wire cooling rack

- Roasting pan

- Hand mixer

- Immersion blender

- Food processor

Utensils and smaller items:

- Knives with knife guards

- Spatulas

- Tongs

- Spoons

- Instant-read thermometer

- Scissors

- Whisk

- Measuring cups and spoons

- Can opener

- Wine opener

- Vegetable peeler

- Zester

- Potato masher

- Microplane grater and regular grater

- Two kitchen timers

- Kitchen twine

As a personal chef, you will be providing a complete cooking service for your clients. Not only will you need to take the supplies you need to cook your meals, you will also need to provide disposable items to package leftovers. Here are some of the disposable items you will want to include in your portable kitchen:

- Aluminum foil

- Plastic wrap

- Vacuum seal bags

- Gallon and quart-size freezer bags

- Disposable containers to hold your finished meals

As a professional personal chef, you are cooking for people who do not have time to prepare their own meals. The clean up that goes on after the meal is prepared can be time consuming. So not only do you need to take a portable kitchen kit to your client's home, you will also need a clean-up kit. The old rule of leaving a place better than you found it definitely applies to personal chefs. Below is a list of some of the items you will need in your cleaning kit:

- Liquid dish soap

- Dishwasher soap packets

- Rubber gloves

- Scrub brush or sponge

- Grease-cutting kitchen cleaner

- Glass cleaner

- Antibacterial cleaner

- Paper towels

- Garbage bags

As a personal chef, you will be doing the shopping to get the items you need to prepare your clients' meals. However, there are some basic food items you will need to keep on hand. These essentials might vary based on your cooking specialization, but here are some ideas to help you start your personal pantry:

- Canola oil

- Olive oil

- Non-stick cooking spray

- Sea salt or kosher salt

- Peppercorns in a peppermill

- Stone ground mustard

- Dijon mustard

- Soy sauce

- Tomato sauce

- Crushed tomatoes

- Tomato paste

- Good-quality, low-sodium chicken broth

- A variety of pastas

- A variety of rice

- Honey

- Sugar

- Flour

- Cornstarch

- Vanilla extract

- Selection of spices and dried herbs

- Panko breadcrumbs

- Balsamic vinegar

- Apple cider vinegar

- Red wine vinegar

Another critical tool you will need, as a professional personal chef, is the knowledge of food safety and proper sanitation. If you have ever had food poisoning, you have witnessed first hand what can happen if food is handled carelessly or improperly.

Your clients have placed their trust in you. They have allowed you to come into their home and prepare all their meals each week. If they were to get food poisoning from just one of your meals, you could lose them as a client.

Be aware that some states may require you to take a proper santitation course and certifiaction to become a personal chef. You will need to display this to your clients.

One of the most important safety precautions, when working

with food, is hand washing. Be sure to take antibacterial soap and a nailbrush with you when you are traveling to each client's kitchen.

Hands should be washed before cooking. You should also be sure to wash your hands periodically during cooking and after cooking. Hands should be washed after using the restroom, smoking, touching your hair, touching your eyes, sneezing or coughing, or handling raw meat.

Disposable gloves can also be used while you are handling food. Change your gloves after handling raw meat to avoid contaminating other food.

Keeping your work area and equipment clean is also key to avoiding contamination of food. Take more than one cutting board with you, as well as disposable cutting board covers. If you are using only one cutting board, be sure to wash the board in warm, soapy water before switching foods. This is especially important if you have used the cutting board to cut raw meat. You might even want to get different colored cutting boards and designate them to different types of food you will be cutting.

Antibacterial cleaner should be used on all surfaces. Clean as you go, keeping your area as clean and sanitary as possible. Pots and pans should be washed as you go.

Always remain aware of, and work to prevent, possibilities of cross-contamination. Meats provide a particularly high chance for spreading bacteria. Meat packages can begin to drip as they start to thaw. This liquid contains bacteria and can contaminate any food it drips on.

You will also want to be aware of the storage and transportation of raw food while you are completing your clients' weekly shopping. Make an itemized grocery list when you go to the store and get perishable foods last. Separate meats and produce in the cart to avoid cross-contamination. Also make sure that the bagger in the check-out line bags the meat separately from the produce. You can also request that they bag and tie each package of meat before placing it into another bag.

Take along a cooler filed with ice to store meat in on the drive between the store and the client's house. Since you will be cooking multiple meals, refrigerate any meat or highly perishable items you will not be using immediately.

Another step you should take when shopping for your client is reading expiration dates on all perishable items, such as dairy products. Older items, with sooner expiration dates, are often moved to the front of the case so that they will be purchased first. If the expiration date is coming up quickly on the food item, check on items closer to the back of the case to find one that has a later expiration date.

You will also want to use a meat thermometer to make sure the meat has reached the proper temperature and has cooked through.

As a professional personal chef, you have a responsibility to cook your clients' food safely and properly. Keeping a clean, well-stocked kitchen and practicing basic food handling safety will help you keep your clients satisfied and happy.

Where Should I Set Up My Business?

This chapter will give you the information you need to decide how to organize the hub of your business, the place where you will be doing the majority of your meal preparation. The best place for setting up your business depends on a variety of factors, including the types of services you will offer, the types of clients that you intend to attract with your business, and the complexity of the meals you will be providing. At the conclusion of this chapter, you will have the information necessary to decide where to set up your operations so you can begin attracting clients and building a profitable business.

Working in Your Client's Kitchen

By the time that you are ready to begin considering where to set up your business operations, you will have probably started to develop an overall vision of your personal chef business. This vision will help shape all aspects of your operations and will be instrumental in helping you decide where you will set up your business and what environment will best suit the needs of you and your prospective clients.

Most personal chefs choose the option of cooking in the client's kitchen. This is a popular option because it eliminates the need for transporting finished entrees from one place to another. It also adds a distinct personal touch to your services because instead of simply delivering meals for the client to heat and serve to his or her family, you will be right there to add your personality to your client's dinner routine. Many clients enjoy the opportunity to chat with a personal chef while a meal is being prepared – this makes the client feel special, because he or she has your personal attention while you are preparing delicious meals for your client's family.

This arrangement also helps to improve the quality of the meals that you serve your clients. By cooking on site, in the client's own kitchen, you can prepare the entrees and put them directly into the refrigerator or freezer. This greatly reduces the risk of the food spoiling, getting contaminated, or being damaged in transit.

If you choose this arrangement, you will need to consider the best time to purchase ingredients that will be used in the meals you prepare for your clients. If you are cooking in your client's kitchen, it might be best to go to the store to purchase ingredients right before you go to your client's home. By doing so, you will only have to transport perishable food items once, from the store to the client's home. Although this helps improve the quality of your clients' meals by minimizing the risk of spoilage or damage to fresh ingredients, it is still important to follow the guidelines for safely handling, choosing, and transporting foods.

One of the disadvantages to cooking in the client's kitchen

is your initial unfamiliarity with the kitchen, where things are stored, and the oven. You can easily avoid this problem by asking the client questions and touring the kitchen at your hiring interview. You might also want to ask your client whether you may take a few minutes to review the layout of the kitchen and the placement of necessary items before you prepare your first meals for the client – you will likely have forgotten some of the details about your client's food preparation environment between the interview and your first time cooking for the client.

During your kitchen tour, ask your client to show you where cooking supplies are stored. Also, take the time to familiarize yourself with the appliances you will be using. Make sure you know how to operate your client's appliances properly and make note of how much refrigerator and freezer space is available for your completed entrees. By taking these simple steps, you will save yourself a significant amount of time when you go to the client's house to prepare the first batch of meals; you will not have to waste crucial minutes trying to remember how to program the client's oven or tying to figure out how you will fit several days' worth of entrees into your client's refrigerator or freezer.

Because many of your clients are too busy to prepare their own food, they might not be willing or available to give you a complete tour of the kitchen. Although a tour is ideal, if your client is unwilling or unable to provide a full tour, you might want to provide a survey for your client to fill out at their leisure instead, asking any questions that will help you familiarize yourself with the kitchen.

You can also attach a list of any instructions you have

for the client to the survey. For example, you will want them to clear enough space in the refrigerator and freezer for your completed entrees and make sure that sufficient counter space is clear for you to use cutting boards, pasta makers, rice cookers, and other tools and appliances. As an added personal chef service, you might even want to offer them the option of allowing you to clear out their refrigerator and cupboards for them. You are offering an all-inclusive personal chef service to your clients, so they might appreciate not having to guess how much space you will need for food preparation or storage. Anything you can add to your services to make your clients' lives easier will help you build your reputation as an excellent personal chef, and help you gain more clients through referrals.

Another way to prepare, if your client cannot provide a complete tour, is to show up fifteen to twenty minutes early on the first day you are scheduled to prepare food. This will give you some time to inspect and familiarize yourself with the kitchen. However, you will want to make sure that you ask your client's permission to do this. Most of your clients will not be home while you are preparing the meals, but it is still important to alert them of any schedule changes. They are trusting you to be in their home while they are away. As a professional, you must respect their home, schedule, and privacy. This includes showing up on time, even though there is no boss to hold you accountable for doing so. It also includes completing your work and leaving a clean kitchen, fully stocked with the weekly meals.

Another potential problem that you might run into while cooking in a client's kitchen is the lack of needed supplies. The items you perceive as being essentials to cooking any meal might not be things that your client owns or has available.

This problem is eliminated somewhat by developing the portable kitchen discussed earlier. However, you might not have every item in your portable kitchen. This is another reason why it is so important to familiarize yourself with the client's kitchen before your initial appointment to cook.

When you tour your client's kitchen, take inventory of what they have available. If they do not have an item you know you will need, add it to your portable kitchen. The items that were suggested for you portable kitchen are just guidelines. If you have chosen to cook in your client's kitchen, you will need to tailor your portable kitchen to your cooking style and specialization. For instance, you might be consistently cooking rice dishes and be used to using a rice cooker. For you, it would probably benefit you to include a rice cooker in your portable kitchen.

Cooking in Your Own Kitchen

Another option for setting up your kitchen is in your own home. By cooking in your own home, you eliminate the need for a portable kitchen. All the supplies you need are already right there in your own kitchen. You will also be familiar with your own appliances.

One major downfall with using your own kitchen is difficulty in keeping the food fresh. If you are in a client's kitchen, the food can go right into the refrigerator or freezer for storage until the client is ready to heat and serve it. But, if you are preparing your food in your own kitchen, you will have to take extra measures to ensure that the food is stored and transported properly.

Another possible disadvantage to setting up your kitchen in your own home is that you might have to purchase a vehicle to transport your food. If you prepare a week's work of meals for your client, it might be difficult to transport it in a small car, especially since you will need to keep the food cool and packed properly so that it will not spill or become damaged in transit.

If you are thinking about using your own kitchen for preparing meals, you will also want to check with your local health board to make sure that this is permissible in your area. Some jurisdictions do not allow food service professionals to serve food that has been prepared somewhere else. It is better to find out whether your jurisdiction allows this before you set up your business and commence operations, so you do not have to worry about incurring fines or having your business shut down later.

When transporting food from your kitchen to your client's refrigerator, you run the risk of the food spilling or becoming damaged. Stacking trays, for example, can cause food to get smashed. It might also shift while you are driving, further adding to the possibility that the meals will not arrive at your client's home in the condition you had intended. If you are going to be cooking in your own kitchen and transporting food back and forth, it might be best to find a refrigeration unit or some other way of keeping food cold and securely packaged while it is in transit.

Time is another factor to consider when you are setting

up your kitchen in your own home. When you cook in the client's kitchen, you need only to transport the groceries, your portable kitchen, and your cleaning kit. If you are cooking in your own kitchen, you will be taking the groceries to your home, cooking the food, loading it into your vehicle, unloading it at the client's house, and packing it into their refrigerator. This process will definitely take more time than cooking in the client's kitchen.

Although it takes more time and involves the risk of transporting the food, you might have clients who do not want you cooking in their kitchen. This could occur for any number of reasons. For example, the client might think their house is too cluttered or messy for someone to come in and cook. Others might not feel comfortable having someone in their home while they are not present.

If you decide that you want to primarily work in the client's kitchen, but have clients who would prefer that you cook the food off site and deliver it, you might want to consider charging an extra delivery fee for these clients.

You might also need to look into hiring employees to help with transporting food. This will save time, but will cost more money because you will have to pay your employees. We will talk more about hiring employees in a later chapter.

You might also choose not to take a client on who does not allow you to work in their kitchen. Although that might seem ludicrous to a person just establishing their business and building their client base, it is important to remember that your time is precious. In the time it takes to pack and load the food at your home, transport it, and unload it at the client's home, it might have been possible to prepare meals for two clients in their own homes. Ultimately, it is important to determine what works best for you and your clientele.

Be aware of your state's guidelines when determining whether or not to cook from your own kitchen. Some states do not allow this and may pull your license if you are caught doing so.

Renting a Kitchen Space

A third option for setting up your business is renting a kitchen space. This option will cost you more start-up money, but might prove to be your best option if you are planning on doing much event catering or hiring employees to help with your business.

Again, if you are thinking of renting a kitchen space, check with your local health board to make sure you can do this in your jurisdiction.

One major advantage to renting a kitchen space is that it will give you more room to spread out and grow your business. A larger kitchen area will allow more employees to work together at a given time without getting in each other's way or running into each other.

Another option is having a storefront available to potential customers. Your business will be more visible to potential clients that shop in the area and they will be more likely to call you or stop in during business hours.

Another advantage to having a rented kitchen and storefront is that you will have room to accommodate people who want to come in and sample your product. This can be extremely beneficial if you plan on catering for events as well as preparing meals for individuals. If your space is large enough, you might even be able to rent out your store space for small events that you will then cater for. It all depends on want you want and the vision you have for your business.

If you want to specialize in providing cooking classes, renting a kitchen can help. By having a larger kitchen space, you can hold your cooking classes on site. You might even be able to provide classes to a larger number of people at once. Offering cooking classes gets your name in the community and helps people learn who you are and what you have to offer.

However, if you are choosing to specialize in cooking meals for families and want to work alone, renting a kitchen space is probably not your best option. Renting a kitchen to work in will require more in start-up costs than working in the client's kitchen because you will be paying to rent your work space. You will also need to purchase a suitable vehicle to transport food if you rent a kitchen space. In addition, you will have to be aware of all of the potential difficulties that are present when you are transporting finished entrees from one location to another.

If you are interested in renting a kitchen space but cannot afford the overhead of renting the space, consider sharing a kitchen space with another chef or caterer. This option will give you the advantage of having the extra space, but will reduce the cost. Most likely, you will not need the space every day and will be able to easily coordinate your schedule with another chef.

When renting kitchen space, look for a space that already has a commercial-grade kitchen that currently includes all of the heavy equipment. This will reduce the cost of outfitting the kitchen on your own. It will also save you the expense of paying for delivery services and movers to transport the equipment to your kitchen.

Just as you will need to stock your portable kitchen to travel to the client's home, you will also need to make sure that your rented kitchen space is properly stocked and ready to go. You will need the same items that would be in the portable kitchen mentioned earlier. You will also want to add any of the items essential to cooking the types of food you specialize in.

Having a rented, commercial-grade kitchen will give you all the equipment and space you need to start a professional personal chef business. In addition, renting a kitchen space will provide you with a kitchen you are familiar with and will save you from having to transport your portable kitchen and cleaning supplies back and forth.

Another major advantage of renting a kitchen space is that you will potentially have more room, more ovens, and more equipment to use, so you can complete entrees faster and more efficiently.

What to Consider When Determining Where You Will Work

When determining which location is right for you, it is important to consider the vision you have for your business. What do you see as your strengths as a personal chef? What do you want your specialty to be? Do you prefer to prepare meals for families or cater for large events? Do you want to be a one-person business or do you see having a larger business that needs staff for event catering or delivery of food?

The best option for a personal chef who wants to prepare meals for individuals and families is cooking in the client's own kitchen, but if catering is your passion and you plan to cater large events, you will probably need a larger space. You will also need somewhere to meet with clients to offer samples of your food. And, you will most likely need to hire employees to help with transportation and serving of food.

If you feel that it is necessary to rent a kitchen space, run an advertisement in the paper or ask friends in the industry whether they would be willing to share a kitchen space with you or whether they know someone who would. Another option is to contract with a local realtor who can help you find a kitchen space.

The most important thing to remember is that your personal chef business is yours. You have the option to be unique and innovative. Take the time to ask yourself how you see your business and look at the options that are the best fit for your needs.

Remember that your vision need not be set in stone. It can change as you and your business change. For example, you might start with only a few clients, preparing weekly meals. But as your business grows, you might choose to expand your business by offering cooking classes. This will help you open up even more opportunities, and find new clients who need your services.

Hiring and Training Employees

Your personal chef business might eventually grow too large for you to do everything on your own. Some personal chefs decide to operate by themselves for a period of time before considering the hiring of additional employees; others will want to more aggressively build the business, and might want to have the hiring completed before the first meal is ever served. In any event, it is important to know how to properly find quality employees that will treat you with loyalty and respect.

This chapter outlines many of the considerations of hiring and training employees to help your personal chef business grow profitably, while providing valuable career experience for the people you choose to hire.

Finding and Pre-Screening Employees

Now that you have a vision of your business and have determined where you want to work, it is time to think about hiring employees. Some of the people you employ to make your business a success will be consultants, lawyers, and accountants. You might also need to hire employees who work for you and help with transportation and delivery, dish washing and clean up, or serving food.

Perhaps you have decided to be both employer and sole employee of your business for now. That is fine; many personal chefs begin their operations without the assistance of employees and find that they are able to serve quite a few clients before additional help becomes necessary. If you are not yet ready to consider hiring employees, you can skip to the section about hiring professionals and consultants and refer back to this section if the need for employees arises in the future. However, if you have determined that hiring a qualified staff is essential to the success of your business, read on for tips on how to choose, hire, and train the right employees for success.

Even if you have decided to hire employees, you will probably still be doing most of the cooking and food preparation. Your employees will be responsible for some of the other elements of your business, such as clean up, transportation of food, and serving food at catered events. Even though these might be relatively low-paying, part-time positions or contingent positions, it is still important to hire the most responsible employees you can attract. The quality of the employees you hire can have a direct influence on your success as a business owner.

Your first consideration should be deciding how much you will need to pay your employees. Check on federal and state minimum wage and labor laws to determine what you will legally need to pay your employees. If you are planning to hire high school students to work part-time, you will also want to check on the maximum number of hours that these employees can work, how many breaks you are required by law to provide, and how late they are allowed to work. If you have an attorney or human resources consultant, they might also be able to help answer these questions for you and provide valuable guidance regarding whether it will be beneficial to your business to hire students as part-time employees.

Taxes and payroll are also important considerations you will need to deal with when setting up and expanding your personal chef business. You will probably need and want to hire an accountant to oversee your tax forms and make sure all tax deductions are legal and for the correct amount.

The first thing you will need to do is let potential employees know that there is a job available. One of the most common ways to get the word out that you are hiring is running an advertisement in the local newspaper. This method of finding employees could also prove to be your most costly and time consuming method of recruiting suitable talent to help you run your business.

With the current job market, this method will probably provide you with a relatively large response; there are many unemployed people looking for entry-level food service positions in many parts of the United States. When writing your advertisement, it is important to be as specific as possible about the job and requirements. Taking time to put together a well-structured advertisement will save you some of the trouble of screening out employees who do not meet the specific job requirements. This will also save time, since running an advertisement in the jobs section of the newspaper will probably provide you with the largest list of potential employees to pre-screen and interview.

It is important to get as much employment history as possible when you are initially screening potential employees. This can be a challenge when hiring for an entry-level position, as some of your candidates might not have established a work history or created a resume. If they do not have any work history, ask for personal references from teachers and family friends.

It might be best to ask potential employees to call in. Have a list of preliminary questions by the phone and be prepared to conduct a pre-screening interview over the phone. These questions need not be complex, but will give you a clearer idea of what applicants you should have come in for an interview and which you can eliminate quickly. Here are some sample questions you can ask when potential employees call in.

- What interested you in this position?

- Do you have any related experience?

- What hours are you available to work?

From the three sample questions listed above, right away you will be able to determine whether the candidate has experience in food service, whether they are available to work the required hours, and whether or not they are particularly interested in the job you are offering or are just looking for any job.

You can be as detailed or brief with your pre-screening interview as you want to be. The first thing you will want to address when setting up your pre-screening interview and the actual interview is what is most important to you. Do you want someone with experience? What hours do you need your employees available and what is the minimum, or maximum, amount of hours you want your employees to work? If the employee will be interacting with customers much, how well do they speak and present themselves?

Having a clear-cut idea of what types of employees you are looking for will make the interview process much quicker and simpler by helping to eliminate those who do not meet your standards.

When pre-screening potential candidates, you will also want to be sure to ask for their first and last name and phone number. This may seem like obvious information you would want to obtain, but sometimes it is easy to forget to ask when you get on the phone with someone. If possible, print out a form with the questions you want to ask; the form should provide a space for the candidate's name and phone number, as well as a comments section for you to make notes on your personal observations about the candidate.

If you feel like you simply do not have the time to speak with and pre-screen every candidate who comes in, you can request a copy of their resume. You can also accept a letter of interest if an applicant does not have a resume. Be sure when using this method of pre-screening employees that you include your e-mail, fax number, or mailing address for the candidates to send their resumes and letters to. Also, be sure to specify what means they may use to contact you. For example, if you do not want to get a huge volume of phone calls from people inquiring about the job, you can indicate in your ad that your do not want candidates to call in.

As the resumes come in, separate out the most qualified candidates. You can still choose to complete a pre-screening phone interview before meeting with the candidate, or if you are operating on a short timeframe and need to hire someone as quickly as possible, you can go ahead and proceed with setting up face-to-face interviews. When looking at letters and resumes, you should already know what qualities you consider most important in an employee and should be prepared to immediately screen out anyone who does not meet your criteria.

Another way to find qualified employees is to ask friends and families for referrals. Most people will not stick their neck out and recommend someone they do not think will do a good job. They know that the failure of someone they refer could reflect negatively on them and their credibility. Therefore, they will take great care in referring family members and friends to potential employers.

Gathering referrals will save you time when it comes to pre-screening employees. You will not have the huge volume of candidate calls and inquiry letters to go through. You will also have the peace of mind of knowing that your candidates already come recommended and have a glowing reference from the family member or friend who referred them.

The best part is that having potential employees referred to you is free.

Another advantage to gathering referrals is that it might help you find people who are interested in the business. These people might be interested in opening their own catering or personal chef business or might be students in culinary school. People who are interested in your industry will more likely take the job more seriously and see it as a career booster rather than just a job.

However, you will not want these people to take your ideas and move in right down the street, undercutting your prices and stealing your customers. Speak with an attorney about setting up a non-compete clause that is fair to both you and your employees. A non-compete agreement is a legal contract that keeps your employees from taking your clientele with them when they open their own businesses. Some non-compete clauses also specify how geographically close a former employee can set up their own business to your existing business.

Looking for employees through the referral process should never be a substitute for checking references. The person referring the potential employee might not be aware of all of their work history or past job performance. If you are requiring your potential employees to provide references from past employers or teachers, it is still important to call and check references before hiring. This practice will help you determine that your candidates are reputable, responsible, and able to conduct themselves properly while on the job. Anyone you hire represents you and your personal chef business; therefore, your employees' actions will be a direct reflection on you and the reputation of your company. As you build your business, your reputation as a professional can make or break your success.

Some personal chefs and caterers choose to hire family members. Hiring a spouse, sibling, cousin, or nieces and nephews as part-time staff can cut out the expense of running advertisements and can save you the time of interviewing because you already know your candidate's employment history and work ethic. If you choose this option, it is important to make sure you hire family members who are responsible and will take the job just as seriously as they would if they were working for an employer who was not a family member.

If you have a rented kitchen or storefront, you might also be able to find employees by placing a help wanted sign in the window. Please be aware that this might increase your traffic. Potential applicants will see your sign and simply walk in during business hours to inquire about the job. If you are currently working alone or do not want interruptions, you might not want to use this option. This option might also be difficult if you are sharing rented kitchen space with another chef or caterer. The employees of the other chef or caterer might not know that you are hiring and will likely not want their work to be interrupted by your potential employees.

If you do decide to put out a sign, you will need to have application forms available for the applicants to fill out. Generic application forms can be ordered online or through a business supply catalogue, or you can have some printed up at your local print shop. In larger metropolitan areas, you might also be able to pick up generic application forms at an office supply store. If you want more personalized application forms with your company's name and logo, you can also get creative and make your own on your office computer. Be sure to ask for your applicant's name, address, personal information, contact numbers, and work history. You can also include any questions you like about relevant skills and work history on your application. If you have hired an attorney or human resources consultant, you might want to have them look over the application form to make sure all of the questions that are asked are legal and within the confines of employment law.

If you have the opportunity to speak with candidates who come in to fill out an application, it might be helpful to use this time to pre-screen. Most applicants who have seen your sign will come in impulsively. This will give you a chance to see how the employee presents themselves and how well groomed they are. This is especially important if your employees will be coming in contact with clients on a regular basis. You will want to choose employees who are well groomed and will present themselves well to clients. Good employees will help you maintain clients and gain referrals.

The Interview Process

Now that you know how to find and pre-screen potential employees, you will need to proceed with the interview process before selecting your employees. The interview process can be long and time consuming, but it is necessary to interview your applicants to hire the right employees. The only exception or reason to not interview potential employees is if you are hiring family members. This is an exception to the rule because you already know your family members and have some familiarity with their work history and work ethic.

If you are hiring your employees from a pool of people who you are not already familiar with, taking the time to interview can save you time in the long run by allowing you to weed out candidates who are not a fit for the job. This also cuts down on turn-over and keeps you from having to constantly look for new employees to replace the ones who did not stick around.

By taking the time to interview, you can also avoid, or cut down on, the risk of employing people who call in often or are habitually late for work. These employees can leave you under staffed and can cause you and the rest of your team to run behind schedule for an event. Being late or failing to have food ready to go on time can cause you to lose clients and be left to deal with customer complaints.

The interview process can be stressful for the employer and the potential employee. If you are not used to interviewing people, you might not be sure of the appropriate questions to ask. If you are nervous and unprepared, you will not be able to focus on the process at hand, which is hiring the best employees for your business.

The number one rule of successful interviewing is to always be prepared. Here are some tips to preparing for an interview:

- Have your questions ready ahead of time. Remember, the interview is not only a chance for you to get to know your potential employee, but a chance for them to get to know you. It is also an opportunity for you to establish your role and your expectations as employer.

- Know what questions you are going to ask and the order in which you are going to ask the questions. Listen to the candidate's answer and take notes so that you will be able to go back and evaluate the candidate when making your final decision.

- Know whom you are interviewing. Remember and respect the fact that your candidates have invested time into applying for your job and sending you the necessary paperwork. Before seeing the scheduled candidate, take a few minutes to read through their resume or application. You can make notes next to the questions you ask of every candidate and write down any additional questions that arose while you where reading over the candidates work history.

- Be on time. Sometimes interviews run longer than expected, so try to allow a little extra time between interviews. If you are meeting the candidate somewhere for the interview, allow extra time to get there and look over your notes before they arrive. This will give you time to relax and collect your thoughts before the interview. It will also set an example for the potential employee, showing them that you are on time and that you expect them to be on time for work.

Now you are probably wondering what you should ask your potential employees. We have already discussed a few questions you may ask when pre-screening your applicants. If you have not previously asked the candidate those three questions, they may be included in the interview. Here are some more sample questions you may ask potential employees when you are conducting an interview. Please note that these questions may be changed, modified, and some left out completely if your applicant does not have any prior work experience. If you are working with an attorney or human resources consultant during the hiring process, you will also want to go over the questions you will ask at the interview with them. With today's strict privacy and employment laws, some questions may be seen as inappropriate to ask.

- What qualities do you feel make you the best candidate for this job?

- What do you feel are your greatest strengths?

- What are your biggest weaknesses?

- What interests you the most about this job?

- If I were to call your previous employers, what would they say are your biggest strengths and weaknesses?

- Why are you looking to leave your current job?

- May I contact your current employer?

- If you were confronted by a dissatisfied customer, how would you react? Listen to their answer, then ask: How would you handle such a confrontation –

that is, how would you resolve the issue to make the customer happy?

- Tell me about a situation where you were confronted by an angry or dissatisfied customer. How did you react? How did you handle the situation?

- What would you do if you found out a fellow employee was stealing?

- What would you do if you saw an employee handling food unsafely?

- What would you do if you saw a fellow employee being rude to a customer or engaging in an argument with a customer?

- What would you say has been your greatest achievement?

- How many times have you been absent from work or school due to personal illness in the past year?

- How many times have you been late for work or school in the last year?

- Is there currently any recurring issue that would cause you to frequently be late or miss work?

- How would you react if you had a major disagreement with a fellow employee?

- Do you have any physical or medical problems that could keep your from performing certain tasks involved with this job?

- Do you have reliable transportation to and from work?

- What date would you be able to start work?

- Do you have any additional training or skills that you would be able to use at this job?

- Have you ever had a disagreement with a fellow employee while on the job? How did you handle it?

- Do you work better alone or with a team?

- Where do you see yourself in the next five years?

- Would you describe yourself as a leader? Why or why not?

- Are you involved in any organizations or activities at school? If so, what activities?

- Have you ever had a leadership role at any of your previous jobs or in any or your school activities? Do you feel like you learned from the experience?

- Do you see yourself as a problem solver?

- Name one experience that you had in which you helped a group you were working with solve a problem or dispute.

- What experience have you had that you feel has influenced your life the most?

These are just a few questions you can ask potential employees. Another way to develop interview questions is to think back to your own job interviews. What questions have past employers asked you that have stuck in your mind? Do you think these questions would be helpful to you in determining whether someone is a good fit for the job you are offering or for your company?

The interview process is your chance to see the real person behind the glowing resume or work history. A thorough job interview should last 20-30 minutes. If you are working on a strict time schedule, try to dedicate at least 15 minutes to each candidate interview.

The less time you spend with each candidate, the more each question will need to count. When you are deciding what questions to ask your applicants, determine what you hope to learn with each question and how relevant and important the question is.

You may also want to test potential employees' skills by having them prepare a dish in the kitchen. This can be from your recipe or theirs; however, having them prepare one of your recipes ensures they can follow diections.

If you have already employed an attorney or legal council to help you set up your business, go over the questions you will ask your candidates with your attorney. Although there may be certain questions you want to ask to determine whether your candidates would make good employees, there are some questions that might not be legal to ask at the interview.

Employment laws are set up to protect both the employer and the employee. You will need to be sure to involve your legal staff in the hiring process. If you are planning on hiring several employees, you might want to contract with a human resources specialist. We will talk more about contracting with professionals later in this section.

Training Employees

Now that you have hired the best employees in the business, you need to train them. Even employees who have worked in a similar setting will need training. This is because each business does things a little differently. You will want to make sure things are being done consistently by each staff member and are being done the way you want them to be done.

It is important not to skimp on training. If this is your first group of employees, consider holding some group training sessions once you have selected your employees. During these training sessions, orient the employees with the equipment and your facility.

Make the training as hands-on as possible, as many people learn from doing. Demonstrate, then let them complete the task themselves, whether it is the proper way to set up the table or quick food preparation. Be sure to address any questions at these training sessions as well.

Sometimes employers will bring in consultants to train employees. Although this might result in highly skilled employees who have been trained by an expert, consultants are costly and might not train your employee the way you would prefer them to. As a small business owner, you will have certain standards that you will want your employees to live up to. You will also want them to do things by your standards. If you hire a consultant to help train employees, make sure they are on the same page with you and your vision for your company. Also make sure that they are flexible and willing to work with you to train employees who will meet your needs.

Once you have employees trained the way you want, you can train designated employees with seniority to train new employees on the job. Be sure to sit down with your trainer and let them know what is expected of them before training begins. This will also be a time to make sure your current employee is comfortable training another. Some employees are natural teachers and like to train others, while some employees do not communicate or teach as well and do not wish to train others at all.

When choosing an employee to train others, you will want to make sure that the employee is patient and communicates well. An employee who does not have the patience to answer questions and the ability to communicate effectively with others will probably not be a good trainer.

If you are asking another employee to train your new hire, it is still important to make your new employee feel welcome. Talk to them and welcome them on their first day of training before introducing them to their trainer.

Contracting with Professionals

A lot of work goes into running a business. As a small business owner, you will probably need to contract with professionals who have expertise in areas such as accounting and the legal aspects of starting and running a business.

These professionals can be costly and you will need to budget for them when putting together your business budget. When you are looking for a lawyer, consultant, or tax specialist, it is important not to shop by price alone. Look for quality and price.

For example, if you are looking for a Web designer to hire as a consultant when getting your Web site off the ground, you will want to see a sample of Web sites they have already completed. Although one Web designer may be offering to contract to complete your Web site at a significantly lower price than most, you probably will want to pay a little more for another Web site design professional to ensure that his or her work is up to your expectations. This will be especially true if a competitor's work is exactly what you are looking for and is only slightly more expensive. After all, with the growing popularity of the internet, it is essential to have a Web site that is organized and well put together.

So how do you find lawyers, tax specialists, and consultants who will fit your budget and still do a good job? The best and easiest way is to ask friends and other small business owners whom they use. This saves you the time of going through the yellow pages and making calls to find professionals who will be able to deliver the services you need within the budget you have set.

Another way to find qualified professionals to provide support for your business is networking. Many towns have organizations for small business owners. Accountants, consultants, and some attorneys are small business owners themselves and can be found in these small business groups. Being a member of one of these groups will also help you gain clients' and referrals.

You can also utilize the Internet to find qualified consultants and professionals. Web sites, such as **www.elance.com** and **www.guru.com**, will give you the opportunity to post a description of the services you need. Qualified professionals can then bid on your project and provide samples of their work. The best thing about most of these Web sites is that it is free for you to post your project and you do not have to choose any of the bidders if none meet your requirements or budget. This is an excellent way to find Web site designers and qualified writers to provide marketing materials for your business.

Here are some things to remember when hiring consultants and professionals as support for your business:

- Always ask about fees up front. See whether you are going to be charged hourly or per project or consultation. If the fee structure is unclear or difficult to understand, ask questions. If it is still unclear or difficult to understand, seek another professional or consultant. If someone cannot be upfront with you, it probably means they have something to hide.

- Always get a contract in writing. A well-written contract will outline the fees up front and clearly define each party's function and responsibilities.

- Always be sure to read and thoroughly understand a contract before signing. Once you have found an attorney to work with, they can look over any contracts you have before you sign.

- Always ask for references and/or samples of their work before hiring or contracting with anyone.

Hiring employees, professionals, and consultants to aid you in starting and running your business can be a difficult and stressful process. Whenever possible, get recommendations from friends and other small business owners. This can save you time and take some of the guess work out of your choices.

Catering to the Dietary Needs of Your Clients

Earlier in this book, you learned a bit about specializing in specific types of cuisine. All clients are different and have unique dietary requirements and preferences. Even if you have not chosen, or do not plan on choosing, an area of specialization, it is still important to be aware of different dietary needs and requirements and be prepared to work with clients who have these needs.

In this chapter, we will talk about some of these different needs and how to work with them. We will also talk about specializing in these different requirements and how you can make yourself invaluable when it comes to catering to your clients' individual dietary needs.

As you know, dietary preferences and requirements can arise for a variety of reasons. Some people are required to eat a restricted diet to maintain their health. Others have particular religious beliefs that prevent them from eating certain foods. Some choose to eat a certain diet because they view it as being healthier and promoting their overall well-being.

No matter what a client's reasons are for choosing or requiring a restricted diet, it is important for you to know what should and what should not be included in their meals. It is also your responsibility to remain professional and respectful of their dietary preferences, regardless of your personal feelings or beliefs. If you feel that a certain restriction or requirement falls way outside of your area of expertise, or you simply feel uncomfortable working with the presented restrictions, refer the potential client to another personal chef who can better serve them. You will earn much greater respect as a chef if you are willing to acknowledge that certain requirements might fall out of your realm of expertise.

Now we will discuss some of the various restrictions you might encounter as a personal chef. Remember, the information in this book is simply an overview. You might need to do more extensive research into each one of these areas, especially if you are planning on a specialization. You will also want to be sure to ask your client plenty of questions to make sure that you remain within their dietary restrictions.

Health Related Eating Restrictions

Some of your clients might have health related eating restrictions. When these clients come to you, they are not only relying on you to take their eating restrictions into consideration, they are also depending on you to provide them with flavorful food and convenient meals that they can serve to their families.

Many clients might be coming to you because they do not have the cooking expertise to prepare flavorful food while remaining within their eating restrictions. This gives you the opportunity to quickly build loyal, long-term clients by providing them with delicious meals that meet their needs; once you have shown your clients that it is possible to have good food and still stay within dietary restrictions, they will be so grateful that they will keep you as their personal chef for as long as they can. Many will also refer additional clients who have similar restrictions.

One common health condition that you might be working with is diabetes. Diabetics have to closely monitor their food intake. This allows most diabetics to control their blood sugar levels and avoid going into diabetic shock or a diabetic coma. Some diabetics regulate their blood sugar with a combination of medication and diet. Others are able to control their sugar levels by diet alone. The diet of a person with diabetes affects how they feel from day to day. It also helps the diabetic person maintain a healthy weight.

Some diabetics work with a dietician to learn how to better regulate their blood sugar. Their dietician will help them determine how much fat, protein, and carbohydrate should be consumed at each meal. Your client's dietician will also help them determine what foods they can eat more of and which foods they should be more sparing with.

If your diabetic client is working with a dietician, ask them what the dietician has recommended for them. You can also ask the client's permission to set up a meeting with the client and his or her dietician so that the two of you can work together as a team to promote your client's health and well being.

Clients who have been diagnosed with high blood pressure might be required to go on a low sodium diet. Too much sodium in a person's diet will cause their blood pressure to rise. Diets high in sodium can also cause fluid retention and swelling, and can cause shortness of breath due to an excess of fluid around the lungs.

The body needs less than a teaspoon of salt a day. However, with so many processed foods and high-sodium products, the average person consumes much more sodium than that in a typical day.

As a personal chef, you can reduce your client's sodium intake by decreasing the amount of salt you use in your cooking. As a culinary professional, you probably already know that there are many tasty alternatives to salt that you can use to season food and add flavor. You can help your client stay within their low sodium diet requirements by seasoning with herbs, spices, and lemons instead of using salt. You can also ask the client whether their doctor permits them to use salt substitutes.

You can also reduce sodium by reading labels when you purchase ingredients for your client's food. Be aware of how much sodium is contained in the food items you are purchasing. You can also purchase low-sodium alternatives to many foods.

In today's society, cholesterol is also a rather common dietary concern. Although there are medications that can help regulate cholesterol, diet is also key to lowering cholesterol and getting healthy.

To accommodate your clients who are battling high cholesterol, cut down on trans fats and saturated fats in your cooking. This will mean cutting out or cutting down on butters and oils. You can also replace fatty meats with leaner meats. Here are some tips on choosing foods for clients who are trying to lower their cholesterol:

- Choose the leanest meat possible. Leaner meat is naturally a better choice for someone who is trying to lower their cholesterol because it contains fewer saturated fats.

- Buy chicken and turkey skinless or remove the skin when you are preparing the food.

- Bake instead of fry whenever possible.

- Choose white meat over dark meat. White meat is lower in saturated fat than dark meat.

- Avoid dishes with goose or duck. These meats are both extremely high in saturated fats and are therefore not good for a client who is trying to lower their cholesterol. If your client especially enjoys these meats, use them sparingly and be sure to remove the skin.

- Use fish in your meals. Fish is generally lower in saturated fats and cholesterol than other meat products. Just check with your client to make sure that he or she is not allergic to fish, especially shellfish.

- If you are making a dish that requires hot dogs, remember that chicken or turkey dogs are lower in cholesterol than those made with beef or pork.

- Use meat substitutes. Tofu and other vegetarian options are often lower in fat than meats. Check with your client as some people are opposed to a vegetarian lifestyle.

- Use soluble fiber. Soluble fiber is present in foods such as apples and oatmeal.

- Leave out the yolk. Egg yolks are extremely high in cholesterol. Egg whites, on the other hand, contain no cholesterol. Try using two egg whites for each egg required in a recipe, and leave out the yolk entirely.

- Use cholesterol-free egg substitutes instead of real eggs.

- Use 1 percent and fat-free skim milk in place of 2 percent or whole milk. Whole milk is very high in fat and cholesterol, but it is still important to include milk products in your client's diet. One percent and fat-free skim milk provide a healthier alternative to a client who wants to lower their cholesterol. When looking for cheeses, choose those that are fat free, low fat, reduced fat, or part skim. These cheeses are lower in cholesterol than other cheese alternatives.

- Use non-fat yogurt, sour cream, and cream cheese instead of regular versions of these ingredients.

- Use liquid vegetable oils, such as olive, canola, corn, soybean, and sunflower.

- Use soft-tub margarine instead of butter. Look for margarines that are made with unsaturated liquid vegetable oils.

- Limit or eliminate butter, lard, fatback, and solid shortenings. These items are very high in saturated fats and cholesterol.

- Use light or fat-free mayonnaise and salad dressings instead of regular dressings. Using light and fat-free dressings cuts down on saturated fats and cholesterol.

- Include more fruits and vegetables in your client's meals. These items contain no cholesterol and are essential to a healthy diet. Try using fruit for a dessert alternative. You can also offer to put together a fruit and/or vegetable tray for the client to use for snacks. Likewise, your clients will appreciate dips that are low in fat and cholesterol. You can offer these to your clients to use on fruits and vegetables.

- Use whole grain breads and rolls instead of white bread. Whole grain breads are higher in fiber and are a healthier choice for someone on a low cholesterol diet.

- Use pasta and rice for entrees. These items are low in cholesterol and are filling. Therefore, you can cut back on portions of meats, which are high in cholesterol.

- Choose low-fat or fat-free brownies, cakes, and cookies as a dessert option. Gelatins, angel food cake, puddings made with one percent or fat-free milk, and fat-free frozen yogurts and sherbets will satisfy your client's sweet tooth while keeping them on their low-cholesterol diet.

As with any client who is on dietary restrictions, ask whether they are working with a dietician and request a meeting with the client and their dietician. You can also work with the client's dietician to formulate meal plans, but you must always be respectful of your client's feelings and privacy. Make sure your client is involved and comfortable with you working directly with their dietician.

Another possible health-related dietary restriction that your clients may require special attention to is allergies. Food allergies can prove to be quite serious and severe allergic reactions can even result in death.

Before working with a client, it is important to make sure that you know about any food allergies they have. A client might not know every ingredient that goes into each entree you prepare. Hence, a client could easily not realize that a meal contains an ingredient he or she is allergic to until it is too late.

As a personal chef, you are responsible for knowing what food allergies your client has and for remembering not to include anything that they are allergic to in their entrees. You will also want to make sure that there is no possibility of transfer of the allergens from your equipment. Properly cleaning and sanitizing your equipment will eliminate this risk and is something you should be doing anyway.

Do you have any of these eating restrictions? Have you ever been a caretaker for someone who does? Have you had any special training or work experience from which you have gained in-depth knowledge on health related eating restrictions?

As you can see, there is much to remember when catering to someone's health related eating restrictions. If you have extensive knowledge about medically based eating restrictions, perhaps you will want to consider specializing in working with people with eating restrictions.

As a chef with expertise at working with people with health related eating restrictions, you could be an invaluable asset to your clients. As you can probably imagine, some personal chefs might not feel comfortable working with people with dietary restrictions knowing how much the client's health can be impacted by foods they eat.

Choosing to specialize does not necessarily limit you to working only with clientele that requires your specific expertise. Specialization helps you target your marketing and showcase your talents.

Religious and Culturally Based Dietary Needs

One thing that makes the United States so unique is that virtually every culture and religious belief is represented. As a professional personal chef, it is likely that you will be working with people from all religions, cultural backgrounds, and walks of life.

Three things that people take seriously are their personal beliefs, culture, and religion. Their beliefs are a large part of what makes them who they are. Whether or not you understand or agree with these religious and culturally-based dietary requirements, they are sacred to your potential client. It is important to be respectful and acknowledge any dietary needs your clients have because of religion, culture, or ethnicity, whether you agree with their beliefs or not.

Any religious or cultural dietary needs should be discussed at your initial interview with the client. Some religious groups and cultures cannot eat certain foods on certain days or mix certain foods in one meal. Listen and take notes as your client is explaining their dietary needs to you. If you do not understand, ask questions and clarify anything that you are unsure about.

If you are uncomfortable with bringing the subject up to your potential clients, provide them with a questionnaire to fill out before the interview and review it with them. Ask any questions you have and make sure you thoroughly understand your client's requirements before the contract is signed.

If you are part of a religious or cultural group that has particular dietary restrictions, you may choose to make that your specialization. Although you will not have to limit yourself to taking on clients who are part of one of these groups, you will have increased credibility and rapport with these clients from the beginning because you will already have something in common with them that is close to their hearts.

Vegetarian and Vegan Diets

With many Americans becoming more health conscious, vegetarian and vegan diets are becoming more popular. However, do not assume that if you have a vegetarian or vegan client, that he or she necessarily wants low calorie, low fat meals – there are a variety of reasons that people choose these diets. Some choose to adopt vegetarian and vegan diets because it makes them feel healthier and better; others choose vegetarian or vegan diets for spiritual or cultural reasons – many Buddhists, for example, adhere to a strict vegetarian diet. Other vegetarians and vegans choose not to eat or use animal products because they perceive such use to be cruel or unfair to animals.

Strict vegetarians do not eat any type of meat. Luckily, there are many tasty replacements for meat available, such as tofu, which is made from soy, and seitan, which is made from wheat. These meat replacements are filling and tasty. You will want to experiment with these meat substitutes if you are not used to using them – some meat substitutes are rather bland when eaten by themselves, so you might find that tofu and seitan based dishes need to be more heavily spiced than other types of dishes. It is also common for tofu to be marinated in a spicy sauce for several hours before being used in meal preparation.

Ask your client if they include any meat at all. This might seem like an odd question to ask a vegetarian, but some people who refer to themselves as vegetarians will eat fish or certain types of poultry, so be sure to have your client specify what their preferences are.

If you have a vegetarian client, find out what meat replacements they prefer. Also ask them what some of their favorite meatless dishes are. Many dishes that typically contain meat can be modified and made vegetarian relatively easily. For ideas, purchase a vegetarian cookbook and modify the recipes to suit your client's preferences, while adding your own flair as a chef.

Vegan diets are a bit more challenging. Vegans do not eat any animal products at all, including dairy or eggs. Luckily, soy products are available to replace dairy products, and some of the same meat replacements used for vegetarian clients can also be used.

One of the biggest challenges with a vegan diet is that so many store-bought foods now contain foods that are made from animal products, and sometimes we do not even realize it. If you are working with a vegan client, you must get into the habit of reading labels and being able to spot foods that contain animal products.

If you are a vegetarian or vegan yourself, this is an excellent area of specialization for you. Foods can be high in flavor without containing meat or animal products. As a chef, it is also fun to use and bring out the natural flavors of foods.

Most metropolitan areas have a vegetarian and vegan population and have natural, organic, and health food stores where you can find a variety of foods to use in cooking for this population.

Diets and Weight Loss

As a personal chef, you might encounter potential clients who wish to lose weight, but do not have the time or cooking savvy to create healthy dishes that will aid in weight loss.

There are many diets out there. In fact, it seems like a new fad diet is being introduced almost daily. Diets include everything from low-fat to low-carb. If your client is trying to loose weight, but has no particular diet in mind, try simply cutting fat and calories in their meals without sacrificing flavor or nutrition. There are many low-fat products available that can substitute for full-fat items.

If your customer has a particular diet they want to continue to follow, go over the diet with them. Find out what foods should be included and what types of foods they need to cut down on. If they are working with a doctor or dietician to lose weight, ask your client to share the dietary recommendations they have been given.

Healthy, low-fat, low-calorie cooking that does not sacrifice flavor is always in demand. If you have a gift and a passion for cooking flavor filled dishes that are low in fat and calories, consider specializing. Your clients will certainly thank you, and tell all of their friends about your cooking, when the weight starts to come off.

Another way to help your client with weight loss is to offer portion control. Measuring portions for your clients can help them cut down on their food and calorie intake without them even having to think about it. After all, the biggest advantage to hiring a personal chef is convenience.

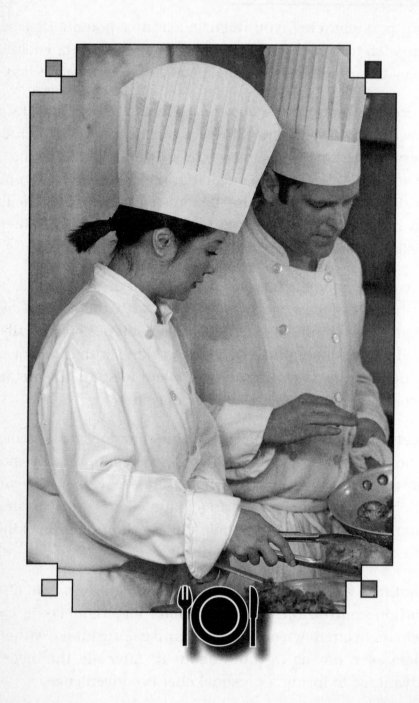

Learning to Cater to Your Client's Personal Preferences

Now that you have learned about working with your client's specialized dietary needs, let us explore the concept of considering your client's personal s and preferences. You will find that each client will have unique preferences and needs that will make it necessary to personalize the meals you provide to varying degrees. A successful personal chef is able to take their client's needs into consideration and produce a variety of meals that their clients will love.

The first step is to get to know your client. Ask questions and make notes about your client's preferences. Another option is to make up a survey for your customer to fill out before the appointment. You will want to go over the questionnaire when you meet with the client and ask any additional questions that might arise.

Although it will take a little extra time for your client to complete a survey or questionnaire, they should understand that you are making this request to help them receive the best possible service. You might want to explain this to your client during the first contact and let them know that periodic surveys might be requested to ensure the client's continued satisfaction.

Here are some questions you will want to ask your client or include on your survey form:

SAMPLE SURVEY

How many meals a month include the following foods?

Beef: ☐   Pork: ☐   Turkey: ☐

Fish: ☐   Chicken: ☐   Vegetarian: ☐

Do you prefer white or dark meat? _____

Do you prefer your meat on-bone or off-bone? _____

Do you prefer your poultry with the skin or without? _____

What types of fish do you prefer? _____

What types of shellfish do you prefer? _____

Do you follow a vegetarian diet? If so, what meat replacements do you enjoy the most? Do you include any types of meat in your diet at all? __

_____

• Do you enjoy vegetarian entrees? If so, how frequently? _____

• Do you like soup as a main entree? _____

• Do you like salad as a main entree? _____

• Do you like pasta as a main entree? _____

What kinds of cheese do you prefer? _____

Do you follow a vegan diet? _____

Are you lactose intolerant? _____

SAMPLE SURVEY

Do you have any allergies or food sensitivities? If so, what are they? __
_____

What fruits and vegetables do you enjoy the most? _____
_____

What fruits and vegetables do you dislike? _____
_____

Please list any foods that you particularly dislike or do not want included in your meals. _____
_____

Do you have any of the following health conditions?

Diabetes: ☐   Heart Problems   ☐

High Cholesterol: ☐   High Blood Pressure: ☐

If yes, are you on a restricted diet? Please explain. _____
_____

Are you trying to lose weight? _____

Would you like portion control? _____

Are you on a particular diet? _____

If yes, which one? _____

What types of cuisines do you particularly enjoy?

Mexican/Latin: ☐   Thai: ☐   Chinese: ☐

Japanese: ☐   French: ☐   Italian: ☐

What types of cuisines do you dislike?

Mexican/Latin: ☐   Thai: ☐   Chinese: ☐

Japanese: ☐   French: ☐   Italian: ☐

SAMPLE SURVEY

What level of spiciness do you prefer?

Mild ☐   Medium ☐

Hot ☐   Extra Hot ☐

Do you want breads or rolls included with your meals? If so, do you prefer: White ☐   Wheat ☐   Other ☐

Do you like soups and salads to go with your entrees? If yes, do you prefer: Soup ☐   Salad ☐   Either ☐

What are your favorite salad greens? _____

Do you have any particular fixings you like on your side salads? _____
_____

What types of dressings do you like? _____

Do you have any specific recipes you would like prepared regularly? _
_____

Do you have any particular comfort foods that you would like used regularly? _____

Do you want a dessert included with your entrees? If so, what types of desserts do you most enjoy? _____

Would you like your meals packaged individually, for two, or family style? _____

What type of containers would you like your food packaged in:

Reusable ☐   Disposable ☐

Will you use your oven or microwave to reheat your food? _____

Is your oven gas or electric? _____

SAMPLE SURVEY

Do all of your stove-top burners work correctly? _____

Do you have a working microwave? _____

Do you have additional refrigerator space where finished entrees can be stored? _____

Do you have additional freezer space where finished entrees can be stored? _____

These questions will get you started. However, you will want to modify them and tailor them to your personal chef business. If you choose a specialization, you might want to create a questionnaire tailored to clients who are interested in your particular specialization.

Now that you have gotten to know your client, you will want to keep the line of communication open so you can continue to deliver the foods they want. Feedback from the client is essential to keeping the customer happy and satisfied with your services. There is nothing more frustrating than losing a customer and not knowing what went wrong.

However, some clients might feel uncomfortable approaching you with feedback or constructive criticism. Some might be afraid of offending you or afraid of confrontation. Others might not have time and figure one meal is not worth complaining about.

As a chef, if you are not hearing any feedback from your clients, you will probably believe everything is fine and keep doing what you are doing, repeating the meal or practice your customer is not enjoying.

Include a feedback form with each week's meals and collect it when you come back the following week to cook. Let your client know that you will be doing this and arrange for them to leave the feedback form in a specific spot to be collected. If you notice that your client is consistently not filling out the feedback forms, remind them that it will help you prepare meals that are more to their liking.

Here are some sample questions to ask on your feedback forms:

- Were you satisfied with this week's meals? If not, what improvements would you like to see?

- Were you happy with the variety of food offered? If not, would you prefer more or less variety?

- Was the food too bland, too spicy, or just right?

- Did you find the ingredients used tasty and flavorful?

- Are there certain foods you particularly enjoyed or would like to see more of?

- Are the foods and portion sizes helping you meet your diet goals? What do you feel are some changes I can make to help you reach your goal?

- Were the meals provided easy to prepare and reheat? Are there changes I can make to make your preparation easier?

- On a scale from 1-5 (1 being "Not At All Satisfied" and 5 being "Completely Satisfied"), how would you rate the following?

◊ Overall meal quality

◊ Variety

◊ Degree of spiciness

◊ Packaging of food

◊ Ease of preparation

◊ Appropriateness for dietary requirements or restrictions

◊ Cleanliness

◊ Overall quality of service

• What comments or suggestions would you like to share? I look forward to receiving your feedback so that I can improve the services provided to you.

After your first few weeks of working with a client, you might want to shorten this form to save them time. The longer comment form can still be used once every four to six months to re-evaluate and track the customer's overall satisfaction.

Below is a sample of questions you will want to include on your simpler weekly customer comment card:

• Has the flavor been bland, too strong, or just right?

• Were the portions provided too big, too small, or just right?

- Were there any dishes included in this week's menu that you did not like? If so, which ones?

In addition to these questions, and on any customer service form you provide, you will want to create a space for the date, the client's name, and comments.

Feel free to include your own questions and structure your customer satisfaction survey any way you would like. The idea of giving your customers a means to communicate and give feedback is so that you can better serve them and retain their business.

Even if you are using the feedback cards, it is still important to leave your contact information with your client so they can get in touch with you. You can purchase ready-made business cards, or make your own by buying blank, perforated business cards that you can feed through your computer's printer. As your business grows, you might want to look into having your name, business name, and contact information on refrigerator magnets to give to your clients.

Although it might sometimes be difficult, try not to take your customers' comments personally. The comments received should be viewed as constructive criticism and are an opportunity for you to improve your business, retain current clients, and get new clients.

Another way to cater to your clients' needs is to let them know they are appreciated. Send thank you notes for referrals, feedback, and for choosing to do business with you. Remember, everyone likes to know they are appreciated. Thanking your client and keeping the lines of communication open is essential to running a successful business.

When a new client hires you on, consider presenting them with a welcome pack. The welcome pack can include a letter of thanks to the client, a biography page about you and how you started your personal chef business, a complete list of the services you provide, general tips for reheating food and storing leftovers, and any other items you think would be helpful to your new client. Your welcome packet can be as unique, elaborate, or as simple as you want it to be.

Customer Service and Satisfaction

Now that we have talked about getting to know the customer and welcoming them to your personal chef business, let us talk a little about customer service.

If you have worked in the food industry, or have served the public in any direct capacity, you know that difficult customers are everywhere. No matter how hard you try, you will inevitably have a customer who will not seem to be happy with your services no matter what you do.

The first step is to try not to take it personally. Your clients are human and many of them will have chosen to hire you because they live busy or chaotic lifestyles. Although it can sometimes be hard to keep a cool head when a dissatisfied customer confronts you with a complaint or problem, it is essential to try to maintain a professional manner and avoid lashing out in anger.

In this chapter, we will discuss some ways to try to keep your customers happy. We will also discuss some ways to effectively deal with the difficult customer without losing your cool.

Creating a Customer Friendly Business

As we discussed in the last section, getting to know your clients and their needs is the most important part of establishing your relationship with them. Each client you have will be unique and will undoubtedly have specific needs that will need to be addressed.

Keeping an open line of communication is the first step to keeping your clients satisfied and happy. You will want to use comment cards weekly, and longer customer satisfaction surveys periodically to make sure the customer is satisfied with your work.

When using these comment cards and customer feedback surveys, it is imperative that you address the client's concern immediately and follow up to make sure your customer was satisfied with the changes made.

For example, your client has brought it to your attention that several of the dishes you prepared for them were a little too spicy for their taste. So, in cooking the next batch of meals, you focus on making the meals less spicy.

Leave a thank you note for your client thanking them for their feedback and letting them know that you have tried to make the current batch of meals less spicy and more to their liking.

Invite the customer to contact you by phone or e-mail to let you know whether the foods were to their liking. If you do not hear from the customer, do not assume that they were satisfied with your corrections. Contact them to follow up before completing their next batch of meals.

As many people get a little tongue tied or simply do not know what to say when contacting clients, decide what you are going to say before picking up the phone. Your conversation can go something like this:

You: Hello Mrs. Smith. This is (your name) from (your business name). How are you?

Client: Good. Yourself?

You: I am doing well, thank you. Just wanted to give you a call to follow up on the comment card you filled out last week. I tried to tone down the spiciness a bit. Were this week's dishes more to your liking?

Client: Oh yes, they were much better. Thank you so much for addressing my concerns so quickly. I really appreciate how much you are helping us out.

You: I am so glad to be of help to you and your family. Has everything else been satisfactory so far this week?

Client: Yes. It has all been wonderful. I especially liked the lasagna. We just had that last night.

You: Mrs. Smith, thank you so much for your time. Let me know if there is anything else I can change or make better for you in the future.

Although you might find it difficult to pick up the phone

and call customers at first, it will get easier with time and it is necessary to running a successful, customer-friendly business.

The feedback forms will work well in providing ongoing good customer service and will certainly help you to troubleshoot problems before they become big enough to cause you to lose a customer.

What if the client has a concern or need that needs to be addressed immediately. What if you find out a customer did not like a specific dish and you did not find out until you had made it for them several times?

To address these problems in a more immediate and timely manner, set up an e-mail account specifically for customers to e-mail you with questions and concerns. E-mail is a quick and simple way for your customers to communicate with you.

You must, however, understand that e-mailing prevents you and your customer from hearing each other's tone of voice or seeing each other's body language while talking. It is very important to monitor the tone of your e-mail and take care that your return messages will not be seen as harsh or angry. It is also important to take this into consideration when you are receiving e-mail from customers. You might feel like they are yelling at you or are very angry with you, when they simply might not have the best written communication skills.

When using e-mail, use proper e-mail etiquette. Using all capitals or bold text is considered the same as yelling when you are writing an e-mail. Also, read your e-mails over to yourself a few times before hitting the send button. If you are wondering about any of it sounding too harsh or inappropriate, try to soften it. If you are still in doubt, asked a trusted friend or family member to read your e-mail. If you must do this, make sure that your customer's name is not showing on the copy you are sharing. It is important to protect your clients' privacy and right to confidentiality at all times.

Since some of your clients might not be comfortable with e-mail, you will also want to establish a business phone line that clearly states your name and the name of your business on the voice mail. If you live alone, you might be able to use your main phone line for both business and personal use. It is, however, important to always have your business name on your voice-mail.

If you have a family or roommates, you will need to establish a separate business line for customers only. This eliminates the possibility of your spouse, roommate, or children taking messages for you and forgetting to give them to you, as well as promoting customer confidentiality. It will also make your business appear more professional.

If you cannot afford to run a separate phone line, some answering machines and voice-mail programs offer separate voice-mail boxes for multiple people. Keep in mind that this does not eliminate the possibility of messages left with family members being lost. It is ideal to make sure that all calls will come directly to you or your voice-mail.

If you have a cell phone that you carry with you at all times, this may be the best number to provide to clients; all calls will go directly to you or your voice-mail. When using your cell phone as your business phone, make sure that your service provider and voice-mail service are reliable. You will also want to let your customer know you are on your cell phone in case the call is dropped or you temporarily lose service.

Whether using a cell phone or private land line, get in the habit of answering your business line with your business name and first name. For example, "Culinary Creations, this is Jane. How can I help you?"

Answering your calls this way is more professional and clearly lets your client, or potential client, know what business they have reached, whom they are speaking with, and lets them know you are ready to help them. Remember, you are a professional and must conduct yourself in a professional manner when answering calls or e-mails.

When using e-mail or voice-mail, check messages often and try to answer your customers' calls and e-mails within one business day. If you are going to be out of town or unable to answer calls or e-mails for longer than that, try to let your clients know ahead of time that you are going out of town.

If an emergency situation arises and you are unable to let your clients know you will be out of town or unavailable to take calls ahead of time, explain that you are out of the office and what day you will be returning so your client knows why it is taking longer than usual to get a return call. Clients do not like to feel as if they are being ignored. Not returning calls in a timely manner communicates to you client that you are not interested in their concern or do not feel that it is important. This is why it is so important to ensure that your voice-mail service is reliable and that your calls will not be intercepted or forgotten by an absent-minded child, spouse, or roommate.

Most e-mail programs have an autoresponder system that can be set up. When you are going to be out of town, set up your autoresponder to let your clients know that you are out of the office and when you expect to return. Some autoresponders will have a general message that will read something like this: "Blank is out of the office January 5th-7th. He/she will be returning to the office on Wednesday, January 8th."

If possible, set up your own personalized message on your autoresponder. This will personalize the message and will give your clients the information they will need about when they may expect your response.

If possible, leave an emergency contact number when going out of town, but let your client know it is to be used for emergency purposes only. As a small business owner, you are entitled to take breaks and vacations. But, by being your own boss, and sole employee in some cases, you hold the sole responsibility for making your business work.

Never wait to call your customer back because you are afraid of confrontation. You have probably had situations in your own personal business dealings when people have not called you back. When business calls are not returned, people are left feeling like they are unappreciated. This only makes the problem worse if they were angry to begin with.

When a client becomes upset or unhappy with the way you have treated them or the way you have done business, one thing is for sure – they will tell their friends. Would you choose to do business with someone whom a friend had a bad experience with? You would probably not want to risk having a similar negative experience to the one your friend had. It will be the same for your customers.

It is critical to your business to address issues and try to find a resolution as soon as possible. Most situations can be resolved if they are handled properly and in a timely manner. Providing opportunities for your clients to provide feedback, keeping the lines or communication open, and returning calls in a timely manner are all essential ingredients to setting up a customer-friendly business.

What Do I Do When One of My Clients Ends Service?

No matter how successful you are or how many people enjoy your food and your services, there will come a time when a client will decide to discontinue using your services. To a creative person such as a personal chef, this can seem like a huge ego blow. Fortunately, there are steps you can take to minimize the impact of a client's departure so that you do not let it distract you from your career goals and your work.

The first thing to remember when a customer decides to end their business agreement with you is not to take it personally. Your clients might choose to end service for any number of reasons. Most of the time, the reason has nothing to do with you. This is especially true if your client has been filling out their comment cards consistently and has never indicated that they have had any problem with their service.

When your client informs you that they are canceling their service, politely respond, "I am sorry to hear that. I will really miss working with you. Is their anything I can do to change your mind?" Responding in this manner lets your client know that you have enjoyed working with them and probes them for information on why they are canceling their contract.

It also shows that you are willing to work with them to resolve any issue they might have with your services. You do not want the customer to leave unhappy with your services when a resolution could have been reached. Sometimes customers are afraid to tell you they are unhappy for fear that of confrontation or because they are afraid they will hurt your feelings.

While it is impossible to please everyone all the time, it is important to do the best you can to leave things on as good of terms as possible. Do the best you can to make things right and move on. If the customer refuses to try to resolve any issues, know that you have done the best you could and let it go.

Most of you customers will probably cancel because their lifestyle has changed and they do not need, or cannot afford, the services of a personal chef any longer. Others will leave due to relocation to another city, marriage, divorce, or a new job. In these situations, thank the client for allowing you to work with them and let them know that they can come back to you in the future if the need for a personal chef should ever arise again. Leave copies of your card with them and tell them that if they know anyone who needs a personal chef, to send them your way. After all, word of mouth and referrals will probably prove to be your least expensive and most effective ways to gain clients.

Customer Service Do's and Don'ts

Now that we have talked about opening up lines of communication for customers and how to properly respond when a customer cancels service, we will look at basic customer service and some specific things to do – and what not to do – when working with customers.

You might be thinking that as long as you are an excellent chef and deliver what your customer asked for, you will not have to worry about irate or dissatisfied customers. However, you will find that excellent customer service skills are just as important to your business as the food you cook and the advertising and marketing you handle.

Then there is the difficult customer. If you have worked with the public at all, you have probably encountered a few in your time. For those of you who have never encountered a difficult customer, get ready, because you are bound to run across one as a business owner.

Difficult customers are the customers who never seem to be satisfied, no matter what. They do not always yell, but are somehow able to make you feel like you are about two inches tall. As with any customer, try not to take it personally.

Some difficult customers do not even realize they are being difficult. They seem to be completely oblivious to the fact that they have made a hurtful comment or have made anyone feel bad. This type of difficult customer has simply never learned to communicate effectively or use tact when communicating with others.

This is not to say that you should ignore them or not take their suggestions seriously. As with any customer, their feelings and opinions count. Try not to become angry or defensive. Politely ask them what they would like for you to change and handle it like you would with any other customer.

Try to remember that this is simply the way this person is and how they communicate. It has nothing to do with you or what this person thinks of you. They simply have never learned to get their point across properly and effectively.

Another type of difficult customer you might encounter is the explosive customer. With this type of customer, everything in their life is wrong all the time. They thrive on conflict and drama and do not seem to know how to communicate without yelling or becoming abrasive.

Again, do not take it personally. With this type of customer, something has to be wrong all the time or they are not happy. If they lash out at you, you are probably simply in the wrong place at the wrong time and have stepped into their line of fire.

Never yell back at this, or any other customer. Yelling back will only create a more volatile situation and will make coming to a resolution less possible. Instead, step back and be the bigger person. Respond to them in a calm and soft tone. Let them know that you are sorry they are upset and that you will do anything that you can to resolve the situation.

If they simply refuse to calm down and continue to yell, scream, and use foul language with you and you cannot get a word in edgewise, end the conversation. Do this as politely as possible. If you are on the phone with the person, do not simply hang up. Tell them that you are sorry they are upset and that you are trying to help them. Tell them that you can tell that they are very angry and you would prefer to discuss this with them later.

Please note, this tactic should be used as a last resort. Whenever possible, try to resolve the problem with the customer as soon as possible. Never simply hang up on them or yell back at them. Only ask to discuss the situation with them later if they are yelling, using foul language, or are acting so unreasonably that nothing you are saying is getting through, or you are not having any luck calming them down and the situation is continuing to escalate.

A third type of difficult customer is the customer that can never seem to tell you what is wrong. This type of customer is usually very calm and can politely tell you they did not like the food that you prepared the following week, but cannot seem to tell you why. They only give you vague response like, "Something was just not right, " or, "That dish just had a strange taste to it."

With this type of customer, take care not to sound defensive. Begin asking questions in an attempt to pinpoint what the customer did not like about the dish or dishes that you prepared. Ask them if the food seemed too spicy or too bland or if there is a certain spice you used that they do not like or do not normally use.

If you still cannot seem to get an idea of what the customer did not like, go back to your original survey and review it with the customer. If possible, go over the recipes you used and see if there is a common ingredient that was in the dishes the customer did not like.

If you still cannot pinpoint the problem, experiment with some new things on the next batch of dishes and see if the customer finds them more to their liking. Keep a close eye on what spices and herbs you use so you will quickly be able to identify whether there is a common ingredient or group of ingredients in the dishes that your customer is not satisfied with.

Another type of difficult customer that you may encounter is the one who never says they are dissatisfied, but you can tell there is something wrong by the way they are acting. This type of customer is afraid to speak up for fear that they will hurt your feelings. They rationalize that it was only one dish, or that they were still able to eat it and that it simply was not that big of a deal.

This type of customer is the one who will remain silent about the problem and will eventually cancel service because they are unhappy, even though they have not given you an opportunity to find a resolution to the problem.

In dealing with this type of customer, do everything you can to make sure the lines of communication are open and encourage them to bring concerns to your attention. You do not, however, want to bombard them. Leave an extra note with their weekly feedback card telling them that you are always looking for ways to improve service to your clients and encourage them to make suggestions for things you can do to improve your service.

Remember, you cannot force your clients to respond to your attempts to provide them with the best service and meal quality possible; but, you will know that you have tried you best to go the extra mile to make your client happy, despite their response, or lack of one.

Here are some customer service Do's and Do Not's that can be used for any customer, even the most difficult ones:

- **Do** make sure that you have a way for your customer to contact you at all times. Nothing is more frustrating than employing someone to provide a service for you and not being able to get in touch with them after the ink dries on the contract. Remember, in your line of work, you might rarely get the opportunity to have a face-to-face conversation with your clients. Therefore, you will need to go the extra mile to make sure they know you are there to address any concerns they might have.

- **Do Not** take criticism or an irate customer personally. Often times, your clients are going to be very busy people. If they are having a bad day or things are not going well for them, they might take it out on you. **Do** respond to them in a calm and professional manner and let them know you are willing to work with them to resolve whatever issue they have with your services.

- **Do** offer resolutions to client concerns and try to reach an agreement with clients when they are dissatisfied with food or service.

- **Do** return phone calls and answer correspondence as quickly as possible. Your clients want to be treated with courtesy and respect and will expect you to address their concerns in a timely manner. Calls should be returned, and e-mails should be answered, the same day they are received, if at all possible.

- **Do Not** put off calling a customer because you are afraid of a confrontation. The longer your customer waits to hear from you, the angrier they will get. Do be prepared to provide resolutions or suggestions to help resolve their problem.

- **Do Not** hang up on a customer if they become irate on the phone. Instead, ask them if it would be better to discuss their problem later. Let them know that you will do your best to resolve their issue, but you cannot help them if they are yelling at you and using foul language.

- **Do Not** yell back at your customer. Yelling or trying to talk over your customer will only make them angrier and will result in an even more volatile situation. **Do** respond to your customer in a calm, soothing tone and try to calm them down so you can get to the root of the problem. Most customer complaints can be resolved favorably if they are handled quickly and calmly.

- **Do** know when it is time to end a relationship with a client or let a client go. Sometimes, no matter how hard you try, there will be people who you will not be able to satisfy. Everyone is different and sometimes personalities clash. **Do Not** take it personally if you cannot resolve an issue with a customer. As long as you have done everything possible to try to make the customer happy and resolve the issue, know that you have done the right thing.

- **Do** try to leave things on as positive a note as you possibly can. **Do Not** become angry with a customer for canceling your service, or quit doing the best job possible because you know you will not be working with them much longer.

- **Do** get to know your customer when you begin service with them. Have them fill out a survey or interview them to determine their likes and dislikes.

- **Do** leave your customer a comment card with each batch of meals. This will encourage your customers to leave feedback and let you know immediately if they are dissatisfied with a meal or batch of meals. **Do** review the feedback forms and try to resolve problems as quickly as possible.

- **Do** follow up with customers and make sure that any changes you made were satisfactory. This will show your client that you are listening to what they want and trying to provide them with the best possible service.

- **Do Not** shrug off or ignore feedback left on a comment card because you see it as being small or unimportant. If it was not important to your customer, they would not have bothered to make note of it.

- **Do Not** assume that since you are not getting any feedback from a customer, they are completely satisfied with your service. Some customers might be afraid to give feedback for fear that they will make you angry or hurt your feelings. If a customer is consistently not providing feedback, do encourage them to do so.

- **Do** remember that excellent customer service is essential to running a successful business. What people in the community are saying about your business plays a huge factor in whether or not you will be successful.

- **Do** ask customers why they are leaving and if there was anything you could have done better, when they end services.

- **Do** know that the customer is always right in their own mind. If the customer is unhappy, it is up to you to address the problem and try to handle it in the most professional way possible.

- **Do Not** become defensive or argumentative when a customer leaves negative feedback or asks you to change something, whether you agree with them or not. Becoming defensive will send the message that your customers cannot be open and honest with you.

- **Do** treat customers the way you would want to be treated. Can you remember times when you experienced excellent customer service? How did that make you feel? Undoubtedly a lot better than the way you felt when you think back to poor customer service experiences that you have had. You have probably had situations where you have chosen never to do business with a certain business again, simply because their customer service was poor. Keep in mind that it will be the same for your clients.

Turning Unhappy Customers into Happy Customers

As you have probably already determined, the ideal situation in solving a customer complaint is to find a resolution that will transform the unhappy customer into a happy customer. In this section, we will look at ways to help the unhappy customer leave the table happy.

It is inevitable that you will have customers who will not be completely satisfied with your services. We have already discussed the do's and do not's of customer service. Now let us look at the customer service process from start to finish by using some different examples.

Case One: You have just completed your first set of dishes for a new customer and already they have contacted you to let you know that their first meal was extremely bland and was not to their liking at all. You are a bit taken aback, because they indicated in their initial interview that they did not care for spicy foods at all. You are also a little surprised that they have contacted you after trying only one meal. They are being polite about it, but you can tell that they are very upset their first meal was such a disappointment.

You are disappointed as well, afraid that you may lose the customers and also feeling that you are not going to be able to please them. So, what will you do? How will you respond to transform them from unhappy to a happy customer?

In this situation, you can offer the client two options and let them choose the option that will work best for them. You can suggest that they try a couple more meals and see if they are more to their liking. Perhaps it was just the particular dish that they chose for their first meal. If they do not like the second meal that they try, offer to provide replacement meals for the remainder of the week.

If they find that option completely unacceptable, offer to provide replacement meals for the remainder of the week. You will want to be careful with offering this option, however. Providing replacement meals might keep the customer happy and retain the business for you, but providing replacement meals is expensive for you as the money for the replacement meals will come out of your pocket. If a customer is continuously asking for replacement meals because they are unhappy with the way the meals have been prepared, consider parting ways with that client.

Case Two: A long-time customer of yours has started to

act strangely with you. They have quit filling out their comment cards. You have left reminder notes and have sent a couple of e-mails asking if they were still satisfied with the meals and service you have been providing. You have also suggested meeting face to face to talk about how you can better serve them. Your client has so far ignored all of your notes and e-mails and has still not been filling out comment cards. In the past, you have had good communication with this customer and they have always willingly offered feedback. You fear that they are no longer happy with your services and are about to leave.

You know that you need to open up the lines of communication with this customer as soon as possible. What will be your next step to get your customer to open up to you? How can you turn this unhappy customer into a happy customer?

Notes and e-mails have been ineffective in reaching out to this customer. It is time to make a phone call. You will want to be sure to have some idea of what to say to your customer before picking up the phone. Open your discussion in a light and friendly, yet professional, manner. Ask them how they are doing, then shift the conversation to the purpose of your call. Let them know that you are concerned that you have not been receiving feedback from them and just wanted to make sure they were completely happy with your service.

It is possible that the customer will let you know that they have just been busy and that they simply have not had time to respond to your notes or e-mails. But, if there is a problem, offer to meet with the customer in person or ask them for suggestions on changes that can be made to better suit them. Remember, if the customer does decide to end services, do not take it personally. You will have made every effort possible to work with the customer to resolve the problem.

Case Three: You have been working with a customer for about six months. They have always provided you with feedback and have always seemed completely satisfied with your meals and your service.

You arrive at the client's home on Wednesday, your regular day to cook for them, and instead of a completed comment card for the previous week's meals, you find a note notifying you that they will no longer be requiring your services as of the end of the month.

You are shocked. These clients have always seemed pleased with your services and you are surprised and a hurt that they are canceling service. You proceed to cook the meals for that week and take even greater care to get everything just right.

What you do next? What will you do to make sure you leave the relationship with this customer on the best terms possible?

In this situation, it is probably hard not to take it personally, but that is what you must do. Try to get in touch with the customer, preferably by phone, immediately. As with any call to an unhappy customer, be calm and professional in your approach. Avoid getting defensive or angry. Calmly let them know that you received their notice. Let them know that you are sorry to see them go and ask if there was anything you could have done better.

In a situation like this, where the customer has been satisfied with your services all along, they might be leaving for reasons totally unrelated to you. Having a personal chef is an extra expense in a family's budget. Job changes or loss, a reduction in hours or overtime at work, divorce, and relocation are all possible reasons that a customer might need to end their service with you. When dealing with this type of situation, try not to jump to conclusions or automatically assume the worst.

If your customer is leaving because they are unsatisfied with your service, see whether they are willing to sit down with you and evaluate what it is that is making them happy. Offer to make changes and see whether they will agree to give you a chance to modify their dishes before they cancel the contract.

One important thing to keep in mind is that some clients do need to go. If you have had repeated complaints with the client and have done every possible thing you can to resolve their issues and they still are not happy, it might be best to let them leave.

As you have seen from the cases listed above, when you practice excellent customer service, it is often possible to transform an unhappy client into a happy one. One thing that cannot be stressed enough is that you should never take criticism from a client personally. Always conduct yourself in a calm, professional manner and never become defensive with the client.

Asking for Referrals

As long as you and your client part ways on good terms, it is perfectly acceptable to ask your client for referrals. If you client no longer wishes to use your services because of a change in his or her personal circumstances, he or she will most likely be happy to refer additional clients to you. Chances are, your client feels bad about taking away from your business, and will be eager to provide other clients who will benefit from your personal chef services.

You can approach this in a number of ways. When you have your final conversation with your client, let him or her know that you have enjoyed working with them and are open to providing personal chef services if your client's circumstances ever change. Let your client know that his or her business was valuable to you, and ask whether there are any friends, family members, or coworkers who might benefit from your services. If possible, give your client a schedule of your available openings so he or she can pass this information along to other people who might be interested in hiring a personal chef to meet their family's needs.

You can also provide your client with a referral packet, which contains a sample menu, a number of business cards, and any other promotional materials that you would ordinarily use to attract new clients. This makes it easy for your client to refer other clients to you, because your referral packet will provide your prospective client with all the information he or she needs to make the decision to contact you to engage your services. Your former client will not have to "sell" others on your services, so they will be much more willing to mention your business to family, friends, and coworkers than if you expected your former client to actively promote your business.

Another way to gain referrals from your previous clients is to periodically mail or e-mail promotional materials to them. Let your previous clients know that, in appreciation for their past business, you would like to offer a discount to any friends or family members who might like to try your services. Emphasize that you are doing this as a personal favor to your former client; this will make that person more inclined to find someone else to replace the business he or she once provided to you.

By staying in contact with your former clients, you not only give yourself the opportunity to gain referrals from them, you also have the opportunity to get them back at some point in the future. You never know when a former client's circumstances will change, and they will once again require the services of a personal chef. If that happens, you want to make sure that your former client remembers to contact you, instead of contacting a competing personal chef.

As a business owner, you will spend quite plenty of time and energy attracting new clients for your personal chef business. Obtaining referrals and enticing former clients to resume using your services takes substantially less time and energy than finding new clients, so it is worth the energy to stay in contact with the people who have already used and enjoyed your services.

Of course, you do not want to continue sending promotional

materials, incentives, and referral requests to former clients who never respond or send you referrals. You have to decide on a point when your time and effort is being wasted and redirect those resources to finding new clients or providing enhanced services for existing clients.

Deciding on that point is partially a matter of personal preference, and partially a matter of business economics. If you think sending materials or otherwise contacting an unresponsive former client is an ineffective use of your resources after two or three months, stop contacting that client and focus instead on finding new clients.

As far as business economy is concerned, take a look at the resources that are required to find, attract, and secure a brand new client. These resources include the time you spend on marketing, advertising, and networking; the money you spend on various marketing materials; and the labor hours used to get that client to try out your services and commit to a contract with you. Once you have spent an equal amount of resources trying to get a client back or obtain referrals from that client, you can safely assume that your time, effort, and money would better be spent elsewhere.

Do not feel like you have to spend years trying to get back a former client or trying to obtain a referral from that client to fulfill some need for validation. Your pride can cause you to spend more time, energy, and money than necessary to try to get back a client who has discontinued using your services. No one wants to lose a client, but letting your pride get in the way can cut into your profits, your leisure time, and even your ability to focus on your career. Make a concerted effort to use your former client contacts, but do it without a sense of attachment to the outcome. If your efforts are not yielding any measurable results, then it might be time to move on.

Now that you have learned about how to properly communicate with your customers to adequately meet their needs and retain a long-term client base, and how to handle clients who choose to suspend using your services for one reason or another, let us move on to another important element of your business – pricing.

What Should You Charge?

Determining how much you should charge for your personal chef services can be a challenging exercise, particularly if you are just starting out in the business. However, taking the time to determine appropriate pricing is critical to the success of your personal chef venture. This chapter will help you choose the pricing structure that will allow you to make a sufficient profit from your services, while making sure that potential and current clients can afford to start or continue using your services.

Unfortunately, there is no easy to determine how much you should charge for your personal chef services. If there was an easy answer, every personal chef would charge the exact same prices, leaving limited room for true competition. You will need to spend some time analyzing your business to arrive at your own pricing structure.

According to the U.S. Personal Chef Association, the average price for personal chef services in the U.S. is $15 to $18 per meal. Of course, this amount varies according the area of the U.S., the demand for personal chef services in a particular area, and the number of chefs serving a particular area. It is fine to use this as a basis for developing your pricing, but you might be missing opportunities in the personal chef market if you simply adopt an average pricing structure based on these numbers.

To determine the correct prices you should charge for your personal chef services, you will need to consider a number of factors that will affect how much you will need to make a profit, and how much the market in your area is willing to pay for your services. Arriving at an appropriate fee structure is a balancing act that takes into account your needs and the needs of your customers.

There are five primary elements to an appropriate pricing structure:

- The total amount of overhead and other expenses you will incur while operating your personal chef business

- Your credentials, experience, and level of expertise in the personal chef industry

- The specialty services you offer to clients

- The level of competition in your area

- The demand for personal chef services in your area

Each of these elements must be thoroughly analyzed and weighed against the others to determine the prices you should charge for your personal chef services.

Overhead and Other Expenses

The first element you should consider when developing your pricing structure is the amount of money you will spend for overhead and other expenses while operating your business. If you have completed your business plan as described in Chapter 3, you should already have a good projection of how much you will spend to promote and run your business.

It is important to understand that in the first years of your business, you might not be operating at a profit – that is, you will be using some of your saved and borrowed money to get the business off the ground, attract your first customers, and establish a client base that will become the core of your business. Many business owners tend to overprice their services based on initial overhead and other expenses, assuming that they will be able to show a profit during their first year in business. The unfortunate result is that these business owners are unable to attract enough clients who are willing to pay high prices for services provided by a novice business owner.

Instead, you should factor expenses into your pricing by dividing your expenses into two broad categories – those required to start and build your business and those that will be incurred on a day-to-day basis.

Expenses Required to Start and Build Your Business

Expenses incurred while starting and building your business include equipment purchases, vehicle loans or leases, and initial advertising, promotions, and discounts. These expenses will be high when you begin your personal chef venture, but will decrease significantly as your business gains momentum and you attract more and more long term clients.

For example, at the onset, you will have to purchase a great deal of equipment – pots, pans, cooking ovens, kitchen appliances, and so on. As you begin to attract clients, you will probably find that additional equipment is needed to cater to your clients' individual tastes and needs. However, as you build your client base, you will find that equipment purchases become more infrequent. You will need to replace some of your equipment from time to time, but your overall costs will decrease dramatically after you have been in business for a year or two.

Likewise, advertising and promotional costs will be high during the first year of your personal chef business because you will want to quickly attract quality clients. As you become well known in your service area, you can decrease your expenditures for marketing materials, radio and television advertisements, and promotional activities.

Recurring Expenses

Recurring expenses include the cost of purchasing ingredients and containers for the meals you prepare, the salaries of you and your employees, the rent or lease of your cooking or food storage space (if you prepare your meals or store ingredients somewhere other than the clients' homes), fuel costs for delivering meals to clients, and maintenance expenses for your delivery vehicles and large kitchen appliances.

These expenses will typically increase as you take on more clients and build your business, so there is a direct correlation between the size of your business and your recurring expenses.

When calculating the overall expenses for the purpose of determining pricing, you should determine the total "business building" expenses over a certain period of time (usually three to five years) and divide that amount over the number of units you anticipate selling during the same time period. For example, if your total equipment, vehicle purchase, and advertising costs over the first three years of your business will be $30,000, and you project selling 15,000 meals over those three years, you would want to factor $2 for equipment costs into the price of each meal.

Because recurring expenses are directly related to the number of meals you sell, they are much easier to calculate when determining your pricing. If you have determined that you will spend $90,000 on ingredients, salaries, packaging, fuel, and maintenance costs to produce and deliver 15,000 meals over a three-year period, you will want to factor $6 into the price of each meal you prepare and deliver to a client.

Using the above examples, your total costs for producing 15,000 meals would be $120,000, or $8 per meal.

Of course, if you offer certain types of meals that require expensive ingredients or significant preparation time, you will want to price those meals accordingly. For example, some types of regional and ethnic cuisines call for ingredients that are expensive and difficult to find – you might have to travel across town to a specialty store to purchase garam masala for Indian dishes, or to buy saffron for Exotic French meals. Since these ingredients are typically only available through specialty retailers, you may have to pay premium prices for these items. Thus, you may find that you need to consider $10 or $12 in recurring expenses for these types of meals.

Credentials, Level of Expertise, and Experience

The second factor you should consider when determining the prices you will charge for your services is your professional credentials. If you are able to demonstrate that you have professional credentials, a high level of expertise in the personal chef field, and significant experience serving clients, you will be able to command higher prices than if you are starting your business with no significant training or experience.

For example, if you have obtained a professional diploma through the Culinary Business Academy and are an accredited member of the U.S. Personal Chef Association, your potential clients will see you as a person with a high level of expertise in the personal chef business and will feel comfortable paying higher prices for your services. These credentials let your clients know that you are dedicated to the personal chef profession, and that you are able to provide top quality service to meet their individual needs. Likewise, any degrees or certifications you have received through a traditional culinary academy or business school will allow you to charge higher fees for your personal chef services.

Specialty Services

If you offer specialty services to your clients that are not available through other personal chefs in your area, you might be able to command premium prices for your personal chef services.

For example, suppose there is a large community of vegetarians in your service area, but there are no personal chefs that offer vegetarian cuisine. If you are a vegetarian, or take the time to develop expertise in creating fine vegetarian dishes, you could specialize in this type of cuisine and set your prices as high as the market will bear. Your clients will appreciate that you understand the nuances of vegetarian cuisine, and will be willing to pay premium prices for the meals you provide.

You will not have to worry about having your prices undercut by your competition, because the other personal chefs in your area will not be able to provide the same specialty services that you offer your clients.

This holds true for any other specialty service that is in demand in your area, such as kosher meals, regional and ethnic cuisines, and meals created with medical dietary restrictions in mind. Providing specialty services gives you the ability to set yourself apart from your competition and allows you to command higher prices by focusing on a specific niche market within your local customer base.

Competition in Your Area

You should also consider the overall level of competition in your service area when determining your pricing. Unless you are exclusively offering specialty services, such as cuisines not offered by other personal chefs in your area, you will have to align your pricing with the other chefs serving your geographic market. Even if you do exclusively provide specialty services, you will need to be aware of what other personal chefs in your area are charging because this will give you an idea of what the market in your area will bear.

If there is intense competition among personal chefs in your area, the overall prices that you will be able to charge for your personal chef services will be lower than in an area where there are few personal chefs competing for the same business.

Demand in Your Area

The final factor you will need to consider when developing a pricing structure for your personal chef services is the level of demand for personal chefs in your area. Do not assume that because there are few other personal chefs operating in an area, you will be able to charge high prices for your services. You might find that the lack of personal chefs is due to a low demand for personal chef services.

Take the time to analyze the demographic factors of your service area when you are considering demand. How many households in the area are comprised of two working adults? What is the average household income in your area? How busy are the other personal chefs that service the same area? Finding the answers to these questions will help you determine whether you have found a relatively untapped market that will bear premium prices for personal chef services, or whether you will be working in an area where demand is low, and you will have to set your prices accordingly.

Developing Fees for Your Personal Chef Services

Once you have arrived at an optimal cost per meal, you will need to consider how you will package your services in a way that clients can afford your services, and that you can build a profitable business without constantly having to search for new customers.

Most personal chefs price their services in weekly or monthly packages, rather than by the individual meal. This helps reduce the time and expenses involved in constantly finding new clients. Imagine how much of your time would be spent finding and attracting new business if each client only purchased one meal from you.

If you have determined that the optimal price for each meal is $15, you could set up several plans for your clients to choose from:

- For those clients who will only need your services on an intermittent basis, you could offer a 20-meal package – this would allow a family of four to have ready to heat meals for an entire work week for $300. This could be a good package to offer for clients who only have occasional busy times when going to the grocery and preparing meals would be difficult – for example, when they are preparing for a vacation, getting ready for the holidays, or when one of the family members will be away on a business trip.

- For clients who will need your personal chef services on a more frequent basis, you could offer an 80-meal package, which would free a family of four from the task of preparing weekday meals for an entire month. Using a pricing structure of $15 per meal, you could offer this package for $1,200 per month. When you factor in the cost of purchasing groceries and the time required to prepare meals during the work week, this package could represent a significant value for your busier clients.

- You could also offer a package for clients who will need your services for a party, reunion, or other one-time event. You could use the same pricing per meal that you use for your other packages. You may also want to add an hourly fee for this type of service, since the client will probably want you to be available for the duration of the event to prepare and serve the meals, rather than simply preparing the meals for storage in your client's refrigerator or freezer. Personal chefs typically charge between $35 and $50 per hour on top of per-meal charges for special events.

There are other types of packages you can offer, depending on the types of personal chef services needed by people in your area. You can find out from existing and prospective clients what types of packages they would like to see offered, and then price these packages accordingly.

Now, let us move on to the next chapter, where we will explore some of the challenges you will encounter when transitioning from a full-time job to a full-time personal chef business.

Preparing for the Financial Responsibilities of Being Self-Employed

The first step to building a successful business is to evaluate and organize your personal finances. Today's society makes it easy for people to overextend themselves with the constant credit card and loan offers that are likely delivered to your mailbox and e-mail inbox daily. Credit cards and loans can provide you with the ability to purchase the things you need more quickly, but it is important to remember that credit cards and loans need to be paid back. In the meantime, they are accruing interest, placing you in debt, and damaging your credit score. In the long run, you will end up paying more for the items you purchased in this manner or might be forced into bankruptcy.

Leaving Your Current Job to Enter the World of the Business Owner

The first thing you will need to do is be realistic. In most cases, owning your own business gives you increased earning potential in the long run. However, it takes time and money to build a business. This is not to say that it is impossible, but you will most likely have more success if you take the time to prepare and get your personal finances in order.

Armed with your vision and business plan for a successful and profitable personal chef business, you might be thinking that you can finally leave your day job and pursue the career of your dreams, but, it could take you awhile to build up enough clientele to make the same income that you are getting from your current employer. You will still need to be able to pay your bills while you are growing your business. Even if you have a spouse or family member who is bringing in income, chances are that you will be required to bring in a certain amount of money in order to keep up with your family's monthly bills and expenditures.

The first thing you will need to do is discuss your financial situation and the affect you leaving your current job will have on your finances. Any reduction in income will not only affect you, but your spouse and children as well. Your entire family will need to make adjustments in their lives and expenditures while you are building your business. Loss or reduction of income, even if it is only temporary, can cause stress on your family. It is important to listen to your family's feelings about your decision to leave your current job, and steady paycheck, to pursue your dream. It is also important to let your family know that you appreciate their efforts to support you while you are building your business.

One way to ensure that you can afford to support yourself

and avoid falling on hard times while building your business is to set aside six months worth of income before quitting your job and pursuing your business full-time. For example, if you bring home $2000 a month from your current job, you will want to save $12,000 before you leave your current job. You might be thinking that it will take too long to save that kind of money out of your current monthly budget. As we discussed earlier, you can include this money in a small business loan. However, you must keep in mind that the money will eventually need to be paid back, usually with interest.

Another way to save back enough money to support your self and your family while building your business is to get a part-time or seasonal job. It is true that taking on a second job will take more hours out of your day, but it will help you save up money faster and will help you avoid getting into more financial debt than you can handle while you are building your business.

Your part-time job could even be your personal chef business. Building your business part-time will help you avoid the financial hardship of leaving your current day job to build your business. Another advantage is that you will not have to wait to start pursuing the career that you have dreamed about.

Perhaps you want to start your personal chef business immediately, but do not feel that you can focus on it enough if you are only working on it part-time. In this case, you might want to consider speaking with your current employer about going part-time at your current job while you are working full-time to build your business.

If it is not possible to cut your hours at your current job, or if your current job is so stressful and draining that it is impossible to stay there while focusing on your new career, consider finding a part-time job that will provide you with as much flexibility and as little stress as possible while you are working toward your goal of becoming a full-time personal chef.

When pursuing part-time employment, you will want to first determine how many hours you will need to work to keep enough income coming in. You will also need to determine how many hours you need to put into building your personal chef business. When looking for a part-time employer, make sure they will be able to give you the pay and the hours you will need before leaving your full-time job.

As with your overall financial considerations, you will want to discuss this move with your family. You will most likely be spending more hours working between your part-time job and personal chef business as you are marketing and taking on new clients.

Another consideration to make while getting your personal finances in order is your personal debt and monthly expenditures. Are their ways to cut back on your monthly spending that will help you free up more money while you are building your business? For example, perhaps you are paying for an extended cable package monthly when you and you family very rarely watch television. In this case, consider shutting off the cable for awhile or downgrading to a less expensive package. This is only one example of how you can cut back on your monthly expenditures. Evaluate your monthly expenses and see what you are spending your money on, then look for ways that you can cut back or save money. For many, this might seem like a daunting task. Remind yourself that it will not be forever and that making small sacrifices now will help you reach your goal of owning your own personal chef business faster and with less debt.

Perhaps you have credit card debt that is creating extra bills in your monthly budget. You will need to dedicate yourself to paying off this debt as soon as possible. Consider using the money you have freed up by eliminating unneeded expenses toward paying off your debt one month at a time. You will also want to look for low interest cards to transfer your higher interest rate cards too. Cutting down on your interest rate will help you pay off your balance faster and save money. Once you have paid off this debt, you will have more money available in your monthly budget.

Benefits and Insurance

Another concern you and your family might have about making the transition into the world of the self-employed business owner is the loss of benefits. Perhaps you have been at you current job for awhile and carry the health benefits for your family. You might also be financing your retirement by paying into a 401K plan. Now you are not only giving up a steady paycheck, but the piece of mind that you are properly paying for retirement. You also know that if you or your family gets sick, you have insurance available to help with medical costs. Many employers also provide disability and life insurance for their employees. Now that you are your own employer, you will be responsible for providing these things for yourself.

Facing such a responsibility is enough to make some potential small business owners rethink their decision to start their own business. However, planning and knowing what programs are available for small business owners, can help make your transition to the world of the self employed much smoother than you would imagine.

If you have been paying into a 401K plan, it can easily be rolled into an Individual Retirement Account (IRA). The money that you move from your 401K is not taxable and you can invest up to 20 percent of your net income per year. The best news is that all funds paid into your IRA are tax deductible. You can set up an IRA by checking with your current insurance agent or by finding an insurance agent who specializes in investment programs. Most IRA programs will allow you to invest on a monthly or yearly basis.

Another option that you might want to consider is an Individual 401K. This 401K plan will have most of the same benefits as the 401K plan that you carried with your employer. This plan will allow for a greater annual contribution than an IRA and all of your contributions are tax deductible. Individual 401K plans do not require you to invest a set amount per year and you will also have the option of skipping years. This plan is for business owners who do not have any employees.

These are only a couple of options that are available to you as a small business owner. The important thing to remember is that these plans are out there and you will have options for retirement planning. You can find out more about the options that are available by contacting your insurance agent or a financial planner.

You also have options available to you for health insurance, especially if you are healthy. If you work with a company with 20 or more employees, the company is required to provide you with 18 months of continued health insurance coverage after termination of your employment. This is a government regulation known as COBRA. As long at you apply for individual coverage within two months of your 18 month COBRA period, you cannot be refused individual health coverage. Dental and vision plans can also be purchased to help with expenses in those areas.

However, some exclusions may apply for pre-existing conditions. If you or a family member who will be covered on the plan has a serious medical condition, you should check with your insurance agent to see whether hospitalization or treatment for that condition will be excluded on an individual health plan. If so, you might want to see if there is a professional or business association in your area that has a group plan available for members. Group insurance has different rules and regulations and might be your only option to get yourself or your family member's condition covered on a health plan.

Another insurance coverage you will want to pick up when becoming self employed is disability coverage. A disability policy will provide you with income if you are unable to work due to becoming disabled. This is valuable coverage and you will want to be sure to start looking for a disability insurer before leaving your job, as most insurers will want self employed individuals to have a steady income for a set amount of months before they will qualify for disability coverage.

Life insurance is also very important to the self-employed business owner. No one wants to think about their own death, but it is crucial to have a plan in place for surviving family members if you pass away. Life insurance can be purchased for varying amounts, and there are a wide variety of plans out there. The most important thing to consider is how much money your family will need to maintain their current means in the event of your death. Talk to your insurance agent to find out what options are best for you.

Marketing Your Personal Chef Services

Throughout this book, you have learned about many aspects of setting up your personal chef business. You have learned how to write an effective business plan, how to choose the equipment you will need to provide superior meals for your clients, how to deal with customer service issues that will occur during the course of your business, and how to set your prices to attract quality clients and build a profitable business.

Now, let us turn to the topic of marketing, where you will learn many effective ways to promote your business so that your venture can continue to grow while you are busy preparing meals for existing clients. In this chapter, you will find out how to use the Internet, print materials, and word of mouth to build a successful and profitable personal chef business.

This chapter will begin with Internet marketing, which many personal chefs use to successfully build a client base. Do not worry – even if you have never built a Web page or written a blog before, this chapter will show you how to set up an Internet marketing strategy to effectively attract clients.

Internet Marketing: Bringing your Business to the Web

Because personal chefs typically operate in a limited geographic area, they often do not consider the Internet to be of significant importance when building their businesses. However, even with a local business like personal chef services, the Internet can be a very important tool. You can use an Internet presence to gain customer interest, educate potential clients about the benefits of using a personal chef, and convince people to use your services.

Building Your Web site: Your Online Business Card

One of the most important aspects of online marketing is the Web site. Your Web site is your business card, brochure, and billboard all rolled into one. It will tell your Web site visitors about the types of services you offer, get them excited about having a personal chef prepare meals for them, and give them an opportunity to contact you to ask questions, make suggestions, or request a consultation for service.

Even though most of your clients will live and work in a small geographic area, people who are interested in your services will still want to visit your Web site to learn about the types of meals you provide, the rates you charge for your services, and your experience as a personal chef. People want to gather as much information as possible before contacting a professional to obtain a service, and your Web site can give visitors all the information they need to make the decision to hire you.

Building a Web site can seem like a daunting task, especially if you have never created one before. Fortunately, there are a number of tools that can help you quickly and easily create a Web site that will attract clients and persuade them to contact you to inquire about your services.

Creating a Web site for a personal chef business is easier than creating many other types of sites, since it is primarily informational in nature. You will not have to worry about setting up a merchant account or a shopping cart to take credit card payments on your Web site, because all payments will be taken care of after you meet with your clients during initial consultations. You will simply need a site that will tell potential clients about you, provide your pricing structure, and give examples of the types of meals you have available.

Here is some basic information about how to get your personal chef Web site up and running quickly, with minimal effort and expense.

Choosing and Purchasing a Domain Name

The first thing you will want to do to establish your Web site is to choose a domain name. A domain name is the address that an Internet user types into the browser bar to access a Web site. It is usually in the format of **http://www.domainname.com**.

When choosing your domain name, you should try to choose

a name that reflects your business as closely as possible. For example, if your business is called Bob's Personal Chef Service, you might choose a domain name like **http:// www.bobspersonalchefservice.com** or **http://www. personalchefbob.com**. These names will allow your visitors to know exactly what to expect when they access your Web site. It will also help you attain high search engine rankings so that more people looking for personal chefs in your area will be able to find your Web site.

Because there are millions of domain names that have already been registered by other Web site owners, it is a good idea to come up with a list of eight or ten possible domain names to choose from. That way, you will have a good chance of finding at least one domain name that is still available.

Once you have a list of possible domain names, you will want to find out which ones are available for purchase. There are numerous Web sites you can use to check the availability of domain names. One of the easiest sites to use for this task is **www.godaddy.com**. On the home page of this Web site, simply type in one of the domain names you are considering and click "Go" and this site will tell you if that domain name has already been taken. If it has, the site will suggest alternate domain names and will allow you to search for other possible names from your list.

If the domain name you have chosen is available, GoDaddy will give you the option to purchase that name for a period of time. Purchasing a domain name is typically inexpensive – GoDaddy will register your chosen name for less than $10 per year, and will usually give you discounts if you register your name for two years or more. Once you have registered a domain name, it is yours to keep for as long as you wish to renew your registration. This means that no other Web site owner will be able to use the domain name you have chosen and purchased.

You will notice that GoDaddy and other domain registration sites will offer you domain names that end in an extension other than .com, such as .biz, .tv, and .info. It can be tempting to use one of these extensions, especially if your favorite domain name is not available with a .com extension. It is not a good idea to use other extensions for a business Web site, though, because Internet users have become so accustomed to seeing .com extensions that they perceive Web sites with other extensions as being less professional. Using an extension other than .com can also hurt your business because if an Internet user visits your site and comes back to find it later, he or she may not remember your Web site address if it has an extension other than .com.

Once you have purchased a domain name for your personal chef Web site, you will need to find a hosting provider for your site.

Choosing a Hosting Provider

A hosting provider stores the pages of your Web site on its servers and allows visitors access to your Web site via those servers. Think of it like conducting research in a library – people want to visit your site, so they type the domain name in their browsers or find your Web site through a search engine, and they are able to access the pages stored on your hosting provider's servers.

For a monthly or yearly fee, a hosting provider will store your Web pages and give you a certain amount of access for your visitors, expressed as "bandwidth." Bandwidth refers to the size and number of files accessed by each visitor, and is calculated for each Web page that a visitor accesses. A simple Web page with text and no pictures may use relatively little bandwidth when accessed by a visitor, but a dynamic page with a textured background and multiple high resolution images or animations may use a high amount of bandwidth each time a user accesses that page.

The amount of bandwidth allotted each month varies depending on the hosting provider and the hosting package you purchase. When you are looking for a hosting provider, it is a good idea to choose one that offers a variety of hosting packages and will allow you to upgrade your package as your personal chef Web site grows and becomes more popular. You might not need 30 gigabytes (Gb) or bandwidth each month when you first launch your Web site, but as your business grows, you might need a package that provides at least that much bandwidth to keep up with the number of visitors using your site.

Keep in mind, though, that once you have reached your allotted bandwidth for a given month, your hosting provider may begin assessing overage charges for additional visitors. In some cases, your provider may even suspend access to your Web site until the following month – a very bad scenario when you are trying to build a business. It is a good idea to keep tabs on how much bandwidth is being used by visitors to your Web site each month so you can upgrade your package long before you start incurring overage charges or service suspensions.

There are several affordable hosting providers that offer packages to meet your business needs. GoDaddy offers packages starting as low as $7 per month. You can also obtain cheap Web hosting at sites like **www.ixwebhosting. com**, **www.hostmonster.com**, and **www.hostgator.com** – all of these Web sites have hosting packages starting at less than $10 per month.

Most Web site hosting providers will also offer software to help you build your Web site. Although the quality of the site builders offered by these companies varies, if you are looking to build a very simple Web site without spending too much time on aesthetics, these site builders can be a good way to get your personal chef Web site up and running in just an evening or two.

Setting Up Your Web Site

Once you have selected your hosting provider, you are ready to begin designing your Web site. If you have knowledge of HTML, you can design the pages of your Web site yourself and customize your site any way you like. If you are not proficient with HTML, there are several options you can use to build a site that is aesthetically pleasing and informative:

- You can use Web site design software. This option gives you the greatest level of customization outside of coding your site in HTML yourself. If you have the funds available to purchase a premium Web site design program, you can buy a copy of Microsoft Expression Web or Adobe Dreamweaver. These programs will cost several hundred dollars each, but will allow you to drag and drop text, images, and animations into your Web pages to create a unique Web site that looks and functions just like you envisioned.

If you do not want to spend the money on premium software, you can download PageBreeze for free from **www.pagebreeze.com**. Pagebreeze works much like Expression Web and Dreamweaver, but is an open source program, which means that users can customize the software to provide additional features without violating the terms of the license agreement. PageBreeze allows you to drag and drop elements into your Web pages, create templates to ensure that all the pages of your site have the same look and feel, and toggle between a WYSIWYG (What You See Is What You Get) view and an HTML view so you can fine tune elements of your site to look the way you want. You will learn more about these Web site creation tools in Chapter 14.

• You can use templates provided by a number of Web sites. Sites like **www.templatemonster.com** and **www.Web sitetemplates.com** allow you to browse hundreds of templates for use with your Web site. Once you have found a template that works for you, you can download it for a nominal fee (usually less than $50) and simply integrate your own text and images into the template to create your Web site. This can be a good way to quickly build your personal chef site, although you run the risk of having your site look just like hundreds of others owned by Web site owners who have purchased the same templates.

- You can hire a freelancer to build and design your Web site for you. There are dozens of Web sites where you can post a job for freelancers to bid on, such as **www.elance.com**, **www.guru.com**, **www.sologig.com**, and **www.getafreelancer.com**. Simply post a description of the type of Web site you want and choose among the freelancers who bid on your project. Depending on the size and complexity of your Web site, you can easily obtain a professional, fully functional site for between $500 and $1,000 without spending your time designing Web pages and making sure that all of your links and images display correctly.

- If you want the best Web site possible with the least amount of effort, you can hire a professional Web site design firm to create your Web site for you. These firms will typically design and code your site, upload the pages to your hosting provider's servers, and maintain your Web site to make sure that all of the pages work correctly. You can even use a Web site design firm to make changes to your site as your business grows. Be prepared to spend several thousand dollars on your site if you choose this option.

As you can see, creating a Web site can be as cheap or as expensive as your budget allows. It all depends on how much money you are willing to budget for a professional site and how much time you have available to handle some or all of the design tasks yourself.

Developing Content for Your Web Site

No matter what method you choose for designing your site, you will need to provide the content that will make up your Web pages. Your personal chef business is your own unique vision. You are ultimately responsible for whether your Web site sells your visitors on your services, so it is a good idea to provide most or all of the content yourself.

One of the best ways to determine the types of content for your site is to browse the Web sites of other personal chefs. You can review sites owned by chefs in your area and sites owned by other chefs around the country. Undoubtedly, you will find elements of these sites that you like and other elements that you will avoid using in your own site. There really is no "right" or "wrong" when it comes to Web site content – you will need to select and create the content that uniquely reflects your business and your personality.

That said, here are examples of the most common types of content pages that appear on personal chef Web sites:

- **The Home Page.** This page is the first thing that most visitors will see when they arrive at your Web site, so you will need to make this page visually appealing and informative. It should succinctly introduce your personal chef business and give visitors an idea of the types of cuisines and services you offer and the geographic area you serve. You do not have to be particularly detailed when creating content for this page – you just want to give your visitors enough information to heighten their interest and keep them on your Web site so they will read more about you and your services.

- **The "About the Chef" Page.** You can use this page to let your visitors know who you are, what you have done, and how you envision helping them with your services. After your visitors finish reading the "About the Chef" page, they should feel like they know you personally – this helps build a relationship of trust before a visitor ever picks up the phone to contact you for an initial consultation. Thus, the tone of this page should be warm, friendly, and conversational.

This is not to say that you should not include your achievements as a personal chef or information about your training or professional designations. This information will help put visitors at ease by letting them know that they are dealing with a true professional. However, the content of this page should help your visitors understand how you can use your experience and training to prepare meals that are beyond their expectations and how they can gain valuable hours each work week by using your professional services. Although this page is about you, it is important to remember that it, along with every page on your Web site, is about your customers and potential customers as well.

To help further establish a relationship with your potential clients through your Web site, you might also want to include a photograph of yourself on your "About the Chef" page. People like to see whom they will be dealing with, and including a picture of yourself adds to the sense of trust that you build through the content on this page.

- **The Menu Page.** This page should contain a sampling of the types of dishes you provide. If you have set up weekly or monthly packages for your clients, you might want to include a few examples of what a week's menu would look like.

  When you are writing content for your menu page, be descriptive. Use words that will make your visitors' mouths water and make your potential clients feel like they would be truly missing out if they did not hire you to cook for them. After all, they are not just buying convenience – they are buying meals that are better than they could get in a restaurant. Anyone can eat fast food every night to avoid the task of cooking. The purpose of this page is to show potential clients how much better your meals are than anything they could pick up from a take out restaurant.

- **The Pricing Page.** If you have successfully gained visitor interest through your Web site's home page, created a relationship with your visitors by using friendly, conversational content on your "About the Chef" page, and informed visitors about the types of meals you offer on your menu page, visitors will want to know how much your services will cost.

  If you have set up weekly or monthly packages, clearly list your prices for each of these packages. Also state whether your fees include the cost of groceries. Personal chefs sometimes charge extra for groceries, especially if a client is only purchasing one or two meals at a time, so it is important to let potential clients know up front whether they will have to pay amounts above your stated fees.

If you provide personal chef services for one time events, such as parties or reunions, you will also want to list your fees per meal, along with any hourly fee you charge for cooking for this type of event. Again, if you charge extra for groceries, you will want to state that as well to avoid confusion.

• **The Contact Page.** This page will give your potential client the opportunity to inquire about your services, schedule an initial consultation, or ask questions about the meals you provide. You can set up a CGI form (which will be discussed later in this chapter) to collect information from visitors – the contact information, along with any comments or questions the client has included, can be sent directly to your e-mail inbox so you can respond promptly.

If you do not have the time or inclination to set up a CGI form for your contact page, you can simply give your e-mail address, along with instructions regarding what information potential clients should include in the e-mail. However, you may find that you spend more time asking clients for pertinent information than with a CGI form, because some visitors will forget to include information you need to set up a consultation or provide a useful response to questions.

- **The Special Services Page.** If you offer additional services, such as cooking classes or gift certificates that visitors can purchase for friends or family members, you will want to include a page that details these special services. For services such as cooking classes, be sure to note whether you offer classes on an individual basis, a group basis, or both. If you offer group classes, it is also a good idea to include your schedule and directions to the place where the classes are conducted.

Content serves two purposes. First, it allows your readers to connect to you. The more your visitors know about you and your business, the more likely they will be to trust you enough to hire you as a personal chef. Since you will not have met your potential clients face to face before they request an initial consultation, visitors must rely on your Web site to find out what kind of a person you are, what kind of experience you have, and what they can expect if they decide to hire you as a personal chef.

It also helps your Web site rank higher in the search engines. The better your search engine ranking, the more people will find your Web site and potentially hire you as their personal chef. Having content that gains high search engine rankings for your Web site is crucial to letting people know about your business online. It is also one of the cheapest ways to market and advertise your services because you do not have to pay for organic search engine rankings.

Using Your Content to Gain Prominent Search Engine Rankings

How can you use the content on your Web site to gain better search engine rankings so that you can attract more visitors and potential customers? The answer lies in the use of keywords within your content, and in several other areas of your Web site.

To understand how keywords can help you gain more Web site traffic, it is important to understand how search engines work. When you upload the pages of your Web site to the Internet, automated virtual robots called "spiders" will scan the pages for content and report results to the search engines. Each search engine has its own methodology for interpreting and using the results reported by the search engine spiders, and uses these results to determine the order in which Web sites will be displayed.

When an Internet user accesses a search engine page, such as Google or MSN Live Search, he or she enters words or phrases related to what he or she is looking for. A person looking for a personal chef is likely to use phrases and words in terms related to the idea of having a chef come to his or her house to prepare meals. A user might use search terms like "personal chef," "in home chef," "meal delivery," and so on. A user might also include terms related to his or her own geographic area, so if he or she is looking for a personal chef in the Cleveland, Ohio area, the search might look something like "personal chef Cleveland Ohio."

Once a user enters a search query, the search engine will return a list of all of the Web sites in its database that contain the search terms within its content. These Web sites are ranked according to a number of factors, including how many times the keywords are used within their content, how much traffic each Web site receives, and how many other Web sites link to them.

Fortunately, many Web site owners do not fully understand how search engines work, and so they do not love creating content that is rich in keywords users will likely enter. They simply write content that is interesting and informative to the readers, which is great for people who visit the Web site, but not useful for search engines.

You can take advantage of this knowledge by including keywords in your content. To determine which keywords you should use, taking a few minutes to stop and think like a potential customer. If you were looking for a personal chef in your area, what terms would you enter into a search engine? Think of several terms that you would use, and write them down. These terms should be the work of your content, and should be used throughout your Web site to attract the attention of the search engines.

How often should you use a particular keyword in your content? Many Web site owners feel that the more often they use a keyword, the better. However, it is unwise to use a particular keyword so often that it makes up more than about four percent of the words on a particular Web page. This can cause search engines to ban your Web site from its listings, because it perceives heavy use of keywords as "spamming," or using keywords so frequently that the content will not make sense to human readers.

Most Internet marketers agree that the most important keywords for your Web site should make up between 2 and 4 percent of your site's content. Many marketers try to have a keyword density of between 2 and 3 percent for importing keywords so they can gain high search engine rankings without making the content unreadable for human visitors.

You should only focus on two or three keywords when writing the content for a particular page. The secondary keywords should be used at a density of 1 to 2 percent. Again, this helps make your content readable and makes it less obvious that you are using your content to improve your search engine rankings.

Techniques to Avoid When Using Keywords in Your Web Site Content

All the techniques described above for including keywords in your Web site's content are considered ethical and valid. In Internet marketing circles, they are known as "White Hat" techniques, referring to the old Western movies in which the good guys wore white hats.

Over the years, though, Web site owners have used a number of other techniques to try to gain additional advantages for search engine ranking purposes. Search engines are aware of all these techniques and have programmed spiders to detect the use of unethical techniques, known in the Internet marketing community as "Black Hat" techniques (use of keywords that is clearly unethical) or "Grey Hat" techniques (use of keywords that is highly questionable).

Not only will the use of unethical or questionable techniques fail to improve your Web site's search engine rankings, it can cause search engines to permanently ban your Web site altogether. This means that, even if you correct the problem, you will never be able to have your Web site ranked on that search engine. If your Web site gets banned on a small or regional search engine, it is bad news for your marketing efforts; if it gets banned on a major search engine such as Google or MSN Search, the consequences will be downright disastrous.

Here are a few of the keyword techniques that will get your Web site banned on nearly any search engine.

Keyword Stuffing

Earlier in this chapter, you learned about keyword density – using keywords in a certain ratio to the total number of words on a Web page to improve your search engine rankings. As noted earlier, a keyword density of between 1 and 4 percent is considered useful for building rankings.

Some Web site owners reason that, if 4 percent is good, then 10 percent or more must be fantastic. Unfortunately, using keywords excessively constitutes a technique known as keyword stuffing – using a keyword so many times in a Web page's contents that the text cannot possibly be useful to Web site visitors.

Keyword stuffing is fairly easy to spot, even for people who are new to the Internet. Read the following example of Web site content that uses keyword stuffing in an effort to gain a better search engine ranking for a Web page (use of the primary keyword is shown in bold):

> *Do you need **personal chef services**? Joe Smith offers **personal chef services** to meet your need for **personal chef services**. What **personal chef services** does Joe Smith offer? All kinds of **personal chef services** – vegan **personal chef services**, vegetarian **personal chef services**, low fat **personal chef services**...nearly any **personal chef services** you can think of!*

This brief, 55-word passage uses the keyword "personal chef services" 9 times – that is a keyword density ratio of over 16 percent. For the human visitor, it amounts to a ridiculous passage that has little value and is rather irritating to read. For a search engine spider, it amounts to keyword stuffing, and a Web page containing this passage would stand little chance of ever being ranked in a search engine's listings.

Aside from using the generally acceptable ratio of 1 to 4 percent for keyword density, another good rule of thumb that can be used is less mathematical and more intuitive. If you or a friend cannot read a passage without picking up on the fact that a certain keyword is being heavily targeted, you are probably overusing the key word in that passage. Even if your Web page does not get banned for keyword stuffing, the overuse of search terms is likely to irritate your Web site visitors and send them looking for products elsewhere.

Invisible Text

This is an old favorite for those who use Black Hat techniques. Invisible text has been used on Web sites for several years in an effort to improve Web pages' search engine rankings. This technique uses elements of keyword stuffing (albeit at keyword density ratios that are much higher than those used for visible text), but users of this technique try to hide its use by making the text color the same as the background color, so human visitors will not be able to see it. The hidden text is usually placed at the bottom of a Web page, where human visitors are not likely to notice a section of seemingly blank space.

The hidden text consists almost entirely of keywords without any regard for useful comments or principals of good grammar. If you scrolled down to a blank space at the bottom of a Web page on which this technique is employed, clicked, held the left mouse button, and dragged the mouse across the blank space, you might highlight a block of text that looks something like this:

Personal chef personal chef services vegan personal chef services vegetarian personal chef services low fat vegan personal chef services low fat vegetarian personal chef services low fat personal chef services personal chef services vegan vegetarian low fat

While most human visitors will not pick up on this use of hidden keyword stuffing because they are looking for a personal chef and not trying to find Web sites with unethical keyword usage, search engine spiders will definitely pick up on this technique. Not only that, but they will recognize this as an attempt to cheat the ranking system and ban the Web site from search engine listings.

It can be tempting to use this technique. Many people who try to use invisible text reason that, since the search engine spiders cannot tell what is contained in an image, they cannot tell what color the text is in relation to the Web site's background either. Since this technique has become so popular, however, search engines have programmed spiders to not only pick up on text and background colors that are the same, but also color combinations that are very similar. Thus, using a light pink text on a white background will garner no better results than using white on white.

You will gain nothing by using this strategy and run the risk of permanently losing the ability to have your Web site appear in search engine listings.

Doorway Pages

This is another technique commonly used by Web site owners to try to cheat their way to better rankings. A doorway page is a Web page that is never seen by human visitors because, as soon as a visitor lands on that page by clicking on a search engine listing, the visitor is redirected to another page on the Web site.

The content on the doorway page is laden with keywords – in essence, an entire page of text similar to that used in the invisible text example above. The theory is that the search engine spiders will read and index the content from this page, and the content's high keyword density will cause the Web site to be ranked higher in the search engine listings.

This is not an effective technique because search engine spiders are programmed to recognize a doorway page by the redirect instructions written into the page's code. Although there are some other legitimate uses for doorway pages that are outside the scope of this book, the combination of a redirect command and heavy keyword density will cause your doorway page to be marked as a Black Hat technique. Then, you will not ever have to worry about how to improve your Web site's ranking again, because it will never appear in the search engine listings at all.

Other Ways to Use Keywords to Improve Your Search Engine Rankings

Although the actual content that makes up your Web site is very important for building search engine rankings, there are other areas of your Web site where you can also use keywords to help improve visibility.

Including Important Keywords in Title Tags

The Web site builder or software you will use to design and construct your Web site will give you the option of choosing a title for each Web page – if you are using Internet Explorer, this title will appear in the blue bar at the very top of the page when it is viewed online.

If you do not specify a title tag, your Web site creation tool will assign a generic tag to each page – "Home," "Page 2," "Page 3," and so on. Although this may not seem like a big problem, settling on default page titles robs you of a chance to improve your page search rankings.

Instead of letting your page titles default to your Web site creation tool's default settings, craft your page titles around the primary keywords for each page. For example, instead of allowing your home page's title to default to "Home," you could name this page "Joe Smith's Personal Chef Service." If you have room, you can also include a secondary keyword in your page title – just make sure that the title is ten words or less. If you specialize in providing vegan and vegetarian meals, "Joe Smith's Personal Chef Service – Vegan and Vegetarian Cuisine" would be a good page title that describes the purpose of your Web site's home page to your visitors. It will also help gain visibility for your Web site, since you are including two keywords for search engine placement purposes.

Web Page Description

Your Web site building software will also give you the opportunity to provide a description for each Web page on your site. This description will not appear on the Web page, but when an Internet user searches for keywords relevant to your personal chef site, the description will appear in the search engine listing under the page title.

This description will give people who are scanning search engine listings a little more information about what is contained on a particular Web page. It should be easily readable and should give your potential visitors a brief overview of what they can expect to find if they click on your link in the search engine listings.

This is also another good opportunity to use your important keywords to improve your Web page's ranking. Spiders will use text contained in these descriptions as a factor in determining where your Web page will rank in relation to other Web pages targeting these keywords.

Here is an example of what a description might look like for your personal chef Web site's home page:

Joe Smith's Personal Chef Service – Vegan and Vegetarian Cuisine

Need a personal chef service to deliver delicious vegan and vegetarian meals to your door? Joe Smith's Personal Chef Service saves you time and hassle by providing ready to eat meals delivered right to your home or office. Receive 20% off your first order today!

This description tells Internet users exactly what they can expect when they visit your Web site. This is important, because when a visitor arrives at a page that does not contain the content they expected, they will immediately click the "back" button and find another Web site to visit. The description also gives search engine users an incentive to visit your site – he or she can save 20 percent off his or her first order. Even though a search engine user probably has no idea how much your services cost before visiting your Web site, the prospect of saving money will still entice them to click on the link to your site.

One note about providing incentives in your page descriptions (and in your Web site content) – it is a good idea to find a way to avoid using the word "free" when describing an incentive. For example, if you decided to provide the first meal for free for new clients, you would want to find a different way of describing this offer – perhaps "Your first meal is on the house" or something similar. The reason for avoiding the word "free" is because it is viewed negatively by most search engines – they associate the word with spam, and can penalize your Web site or even remove it from search engines completely for using the word "free" in your page descriptions or content.

Meta Tags

Another element you can include in your Web pages to improve your search engine rankings is the meta tag. Meta tags are words or phrases that are inserted into the header section of the HTML code of your Web page – the part of the code that tells the browser certain information about the Web page that human visitors need not be concerned with.

Your Web site visitors will not see the meta tags you use for each Web page, but search engine spiders will see them. You can use your keywords in the meta tag field to tell the search engine spiders about the contents of your Web page, above and beyond the information available in your page content.

If you looked at the HTML header code for the home page of a personal chef Web site, here is what it might look like:

<HEAD>
<TITLE> Joe Smith's Personal Chef Service – Vegan and Vegetarian Cuisine</TITLE>
<META Name="description" content=" Need a personal chef service to deliver delicious vegan and vegetarian meals to your door? Joe Smith's Personal Chef Service saves you

time and hassle by providing ready to eat meals delivered right to your home or office. Receive 20% off your first order today!">
<META Name="keywords" content="personal chef, personal chef service, vegan, vegetarian, vegan cuisine, vegetarian cuisine">
</HEAD>

Some Internet marketers will tell you that meta tags are no longer important for improving your search engine rankings, and that search engine spiders do not use meta tags when determining rankings. However, since the algorithms used by search engines are proprietary, it is impossible to tell which search engines use meta tags as criteria for ranking Web pages.

Since it is not possible to determine whether meta tags are used by a particular search engine, the small amount of time you will spend creating tags for your pages will be, at worst, a way to easily remember which keywords you targeted for each Web page and, at best, another way to augment your Web site content to help your pages achieve better rankings.

Image Tags

A frequently overlooked technique for using keywords to improve your Web site's search engine rankings is to place relevant keywords in your image tags, also called ALT tags.

If you have ever browsed a Web site and held the pointer over an image and a small yellow box appeared with a short description of the image, you might have wondered why the Web site owner bothered to do this. After all, is not the content of the image self-explanatory?

Although you can look at an image and tell right away what is contained in the image, search engine spiders do not have this ability. The spiders know that an image exists, but they cannot derive any useful information from it. The ALT tag is a way to describe the image to the search engine spider. It is also a useful tool for loading your Web pages with a few additional keywords.

Your ALT tag should be short – no more than eight to ten words – and should contain no more than one or two keywords. It should also accurately describe the image with words that are as specific as possible to the image's content.

An example of an ALT tag for an image of a tikka masala dish might look something like this:

Tikka Masala – Joe Smith's Personal Chef Menu Item

This ALT tag gives Web site visitors the name of the dish and includes the primary keyword targeted for that page.

Software and Web Services to Help You Run Your Personal Chef Business

L ike any professional who is building a successful, profitable business, personal chefs need a number of tools to help them save time and make routine task handling more efficient. Without the correct tools for running your business, you could spend unnecessary hours on tasks that, while necessary for the success of your business, take time away from what you truly love to do – prepare creative, delicious meals for your clients.

This chapter will help you find numerous tools that you can use to build your business more quickly and easily, while saving money and frustration. Some of these tools can be acquired along the way, as your business begins to generate a profit, while others are essential to getting started and will be of little use if you try to use them after your business is already up and running.

You will also learn the approximate cost of each of these tools so you can budget for them while you are building your online presence. When possible, this chapter will include information about free tools that have similar functions to their expensive alternatives to help you keep costs down.

Web Site Creation Tools

Unless you use a template-based site builder offered by your Web site host, or you have extensive knowledge of Web site coding languages, such as HTML and JavaScript, you will need a Web site creation tool to properly design your site and make sure all the elements of your site function correctly. There are several Web site creation tools available that can make designing your Web site a simple and relatively quick process. Here are some of the most commonly used tools:

Microsoft Expression Studio

Microsoft Expression Studio consists of a suite of tools that can help you easily create Web pages, design content for your Web site, and manage your data files for easy retrieval. There are four programs included with Microsoft Expression Studio.

Microsoft Expression Web

This application allows you to create Web pages via a WYSIWYG (What You See Is What You Get) interface. This means that instead of requiring you to manually code your Web pages in HTML or other Internet language, Expression Web allows you to point and click to decide where you want text, images, links, and other Web site elements. While you are building your pages, Expression Web will create HTML code designed to make sure your Web site will display correctly on all browsers.

If you do have HTML programming experience, you can also toggle between Expression Web's WYSIWYG interface and the site's HTML code to fine tune your Web site's design and functionality.

Microsoft Expression Blend

This program allows you to seamlessly place sophisticated media files within your Web pages. You can use Expression Blend to integrate animations, text with high quality and nonstandard fonts, vector graphics, video, and three dimensional effects into your site design. Expression Blend converts vector and bitmap graphics to XAML format, making integration of complex image file types a simple process.

Microsoft Expression Design

The Microsoft Expression Design tool lets you create the media and image files you will integrate into your Web site via the Microsoft Blend application. You can create seamless video, high quality vector graphics, animation files, and more for your Web site. These files capture the interest of your Web site visitors and help keep them on your site longer so they will be more inclined to contact you.

Microsoft Expression Media

If you are building a complex Web site with multiple pages and galleries, you likely have hundreds or even thousands of files to keep track of. Microsoft Expression Media is a tool for categorizing, managing, and storing these files so you can easily find and retrieve the exact files you want while you are building or updating your site.

This is particularly important for managing online gallery pages, where you will include images of sample dishes you have created. Using these images can be a powerful way to generate interest in your personal chef business because people will see the colors and textures of the foods you provide, which will create an emotional need for your services.

While Microsoft Expression Studio offers several powerful tools for building a dynamic and user-friendly Web site, it can be expensive for an artist just starting out on the Internet. You can purchase this suite of Web site tools on **www.microsoft.com/expression** for $599, but you can also find Microsoft Expression Studio on **www.amazon. com** for about $560.

If you think you might want to create a unique, complex site rich with graphic and video features but you do not want to pay a developer to create your Web site for you, Microsoft Expression Web might be worth the substantial investment.

Before getting out your credit card to order Microsoft Expression Web, though, you might want to download a free trial version of the software suite from **www.microsoft. com/expression**. You can try the software applications for 60 days, which will give you time to learn how to use the various features and start building your Web site. Keep in mind, though, that if you do not purchase Microsoft Expression Studio at the end of your trial period, you will not be able to retrieve the Web pages you have created while using the trial software.

Adobe Dreamweaver CS3

Adobe Dreamweaver CS3 gives you much of the same functionality as Microsoft Expression Studio, but it combines all its features into one software application. You can toggle between the WYSIWYG interface and the HTML or XHTML code for your Web site, so you can create your site exactly the way you want.

You can also use CSS style sheets for your site, which are sections of code that allow you to easily make each page of your Web site follow the same design style without having to manually match up the colors and element placements on each page. Dreamweaver CS3 also features a browser validation tool that checks to make sure your Web site layout is compatible with all browser types.

If you intend to integrate video into your Web site, Dreamweaver CS3 gives you the ability to incorporate Adobe Flash video files into your Web pages with just a few mouse clicks. This is a significant advantage over other types of Web site creation tools, which can make video integration a tedious and frustrating process.

Dreamweaver CS3 is also a good choice if you use a Macintosh as your main computer. This Web site creation tool is designed to be compatible with both Windows-based systems and Macintosh systems.

If you purchase Adobe Dreamweaver CS3 directly from the manufacturer's Web site at **www.adobe.com/products/ dreamweaver**, you can expect to pay about $600 for this software; however, you can find Dreamweaver CS3 on **www. amazon.com** for as little as $399.

Like Microsoft Expressions Studio, Adobe Dreamweaver CS3 is available as a trial download. You can go to **www. adobe.com/products/dreamweaver** and download the trial version for 45 days.

PageBreeze

If Adobe Dreamweaver CS3 and Microsoft Expressions Studio are a little expensive for your marketing budget, then consider using PageBreeze to build your Web site. PageBreeze is a free Web site creation tool available for download at **www.pagebreeze.com**. There are no time restrictions or hidden fees associated with your PageBreeze download – you can use the free software as long as you like and build as many Web sites and Web pages as you want.

The software is not as sophisticated as Dreamweaver CS3 or Expression Web, but it does give you the ability to build your Web site via both a WYSIWYG interface and an HTML coding page. It also allows you to use CSS to create style sheets to make sure that the pages of your personal chef Web site complement each other.

You can easily import graphics from Adobe Photoshop, Paint Shop Pro, or another graphics program, as long as you save the graphics in a JPEG or GIF format. Adding these graphics to your Web site is as simple as clicking where you want the graphic to appear in your Web page and clicking "Insert Graphic" on the PageBreeze toolbar.

Adding text to your Web pages is very simple as well. Just click the area on your Web page where you want the text to appear and start typing. If you want multiple columns of text on a Web Page or you want to create a sidebar where you can provide links or featured information, just click "Tables" on the toolbar and select the number of columns you want. You can make the table borders invisible so they do not appear on your finished Web page.

Although PageBreeze lacks some of the versatility of Dreamweaver CS3 or Expression Web, you can easily alter the HTML code to change Web page elements that you cannot create in WYSIWYG mode.

For example, PageBreeze offers a very limited number of text fonts – while you are in WYSIWYG mode, you are limited to Arial, Times New Roman, Courier, Tahoma, Verdana, and Wingdings. However, if you switch to HTML mode, you can change the font to any font that is browser supported (this includes almost all fonts used in popular word processing programs). You can use Microsoft Word or another word processing program to find a font appropriate for your Web site.

Once you have found a font you like, just look through the HTML code for references to the font you used in WYSIWYG mode and replace them with the name of your new font.

To illustrate, here is an example of a piece of HTML code generated in PageBreeze:

```
<p align="center"> </p>
<p align="center"><font face="Arial"
size="4"><strong>Thank You!</strong></font></p>
<p align="center"><font face="Arial" size="4">Thank you for
```
your interest in Bob Smith's Personal Chef Service. I look forward to meeting you in person and serving the dining needs of you and your family.</font></p>

<p align="center"><font face="Arial" size="4">If you have included your postal address or e-mail address with your consultation request, you will receive a questionnaire to help me become familiar with the types of meals your family enjoys. It will only take you a few minutes to fill out the questionnaire, but doing this will help ensure that you and your family are happy with my services. </font></p>

<p align="center"><font face="Arial" size="4">I will bring your completed questionnaire to our initial meeting so that we can design a custom meal plan. </font></p>

Although this might look intimidating if you have never worked with HTML, you do not need to be concerned with the majority of this code. Just look for the references to Arial font:

```
<p align="center"> </p>
<p align="center"><font face="Arial"
size="4"><strong>Thank You!</strong></font></p>
<p align="center"><font face="Arial" size="4"> Thank you
```
for your interest in Bob Smith's Personal Chef Service. I look forward to meeting you in person and serving the dining needs of you and your family.</font></p>

<p align="center"><font face="**Arial**" size="4"> If you have included your postal address or e-mail address with your consultation request, you will receive a questionnaire to

help me become familiar with the types of meals your family enjoys. It will only take you a few minutes to fill out the questionnaire, but doing this will help ensure that you and your family are happy with my services. </font></p>
<p align="center"><font face="**Arial**" size="4"> I will bring your completed questionnaire to our initial meeting so that we can design a custom meal plan. </font></p>

Let us suppose you have decided that Calibri font would be appropriate for the look and feel of your Web site. All you would need to do is replace all of the references to "Arial" with "Calibri":

<p align="center"> </p>
<p align="center"><font face="**Calibri**" size="4"><strong>Thank You!</strong></font></p>
<p align="center"><font face="**Calibri**" size="4"> Thank you for your interest in Bob Smith's Personal Chef Service. I look forward to meeting you in person and serving the dining needs of you and your family.</font></p>
<p align="center"><font face="**Calibri**" size="4"> If you have included your postal address or e-mail address with your consultation request, you will receive a questionnaire to help me become familiar with the types of meals your family enjoys. It will only take you a few minutes to fill out the questionnaire, but doing this will help ensure that you and your family are happy with my services. </font></p>
<p align="center"><font face="**Calibri**" size="4"> I will bring your completed questionnaire to our initial meeting so that we can design a custom meal plan. </font></p>

Click the save button and then the text in your Web page

associated with this section of HTML code will display in Calibri font.

You can make similar adjustments to font sizes, table widths, and other elements that might be difficult to perfect in WYSIWYG mode. You will also need to use the HTML mode to insert video or JavaScript elements into your Web pages. Do not worry; you can use other software or Web applications to generate the code you will need to integrate these elements into your Web pages so you will not have to worry about coding it yourself.

Again, working with PageBreeze can be a little more cumbersome than working with Dreamweaver CS3 or Expressions Studio, but if you are building a fairly simple Web site and are not afraid to fine tune the HTML code for your pages, PageBreeze can be a very economical way to design your Web site and achieve professional results.

CGI Forms and Autoresponder Tools

As noted in Chapter 13, your Web site is one of the most important elements of your personal chef business' online marketing strategy. However, in order to generate repeat visitors, you will need to utilize a means of reminding your visitors of your presence and enticing them to return to your Web site through discounts, special offers, and announcements of new dishes, meal plans, and cooking classes. The easiest way to do this is to provide a way for your Web site visitors to enter their e-mail addresses on your site, and to compile these e-mail addresses into marketing lists so you can create e-mail announcements.

A CGI form is a text field you can place on your Web site so your visitors can enter their contact details or other information. You can use CGI forms to ask visitors for their names, e-mail addresses, telephone numbers, favorite types of cuisines, or nearly any other type of information you can use in your marketing efforts.

Once a Web site visitor has entered his or her contact information into a CGI form on your Web site, it will be transmitted to a CGI bin, which formats the information submitted by the visitor and sends it to your e-mail address. You can then transfer the information to a database, which you can use to easily send e-mail messages to an entire group of people with just the click of a mouse.

Because federal laws prohibit the use of spam or transmission of unsolicited e-mail messages, you should always couple CGI forms with a pre-written e-mail requiring visitors to confirm that they have voluntarily submitted their contact information and that they consent to receiving e-mail messages from you. This will help save you from receiving numerous complaints from people who completed a CGI form on your Web site but have since forgotten that they did so.

Autoresponders are e-mail programs that allow you to compose e-mails and have them sent as soon as a visitor completes a CGI form on your Web site, and at specified time intervals thereafter. This can save you hundreds of hours of time because you can set up your e-mail messages once and never have to worry about checking for new subscribers so you can manually send them a series of e-mails.

There are several applications that can help you place CGI forms on your Web site and automatically send e-mail messages to them to promote your personal chef services, announce discounts and specials, and provide your subscribers with useful information to help you gain more loyal clients for your business.

FormBreeze

FormBreeze is a CGI form generator and autoresponder system that is designed for use with the PageBreeze Web site creation tool. FormBreeze offers the PageBreeze tool for free, knowing that a certain percentage of PageBreeze users will subscribe to the FormBreeze service.

FormBreeze allows you to easily create visitor input forms for use on you Web site and provides unlimited autoresponders to send e-mail messages to subscribers that complete your Web forms.

You can customize your autoresponder messages to be sent at specified intervals. For example, you might create a confirmation e-mail that will be sent as soon as a visitor completes a CGI Web form, a welcome message that will be sent as soon as the visitor confirms his or her subscription, and sales e-mails every other day for the next two weeks to help familiarize your subscriber with your personal chef services. You can also create broadcast e-mails that will be sent to all your current subscribers at once so you can alert them of new cooking classes or offer them discounts that will only be available for a limited time.

FormBreeze allows you to collect statistics about your

subscribers, such as the percentage of subscribers that open an autoresponder e-mail, the number of subscribers that click on a link contained in an e-mail, and the number of people that unsubscribe from your mailing lists. This can help you understand how well your e-mail marketing efforts are working so that you can make adjustments on future e-mail campaigns.

FormBreeze offers two subscription packages: The first allows you to create up to three CGI forms with unlimited autoresponder messages for $6.99 per month; the second allows you to create up to ten CGI forms with unlimited autoresponder messages for $19.99 per month. Unless you have more than one Web site for your personal chef services, it is unlikely that you will need more than three CGI forms; however, if you plan on expanding your e-mail marketing efforts in the future, the second package might be a useful solution.

AWeber Communications

AWeber is another tool you can use to create CGI forms, place the forms on your Web site, and create autoresponder messages to be sent to people who complete and submit the forms.

With AWeber, you can create several types of CGI forms, depending on how aggressively you want to pursue e-mail marketing. Like FormBreeze, you can create a simple CGI form that can be placed anywhere on your Web pages, giving Web site visitors the option to subscribe to your newsletters or obtain free informational products. AWeber also gives you the ability to create CGI forms that pop up when a visitor opens a Web page on your site, making the form the focal point of the page until the visitor completes and submits the form or closes the pop up box. You can also create exit pop up forms, which prompts visitors to enter contact information when they navigate away from your Web site.

Pop up and exit pop up CGI forms can be good tools if your marketing focus includes aggressive e-mail marketing, but they have a couple of drawbacks. First, they are viewed by some Web site visitors as intrusive and might cause you to lose repeat visitors because of the aggressiveness associated with pop ups. Second, they can easily be disabled by a pop up blocker, which is a software application that detects pop ups and disables them before they can be seen by a Web site visitor. Pop up blockers will dilute the effectiveness of these CGI forms because many of your Web site visitors will not see them and will not have an opportunity to subscribe to your marketing list.

AWeber also gives you the ability to create and manage autoresponder messages for each CGI form you create. You can write a series of e-mail messages and configure an autoresponder to send the messages at specified intervals. You can also write broadcast messages that will be sent to all your current subscribers at a specified time.

You will also have access to statistical information about the use of messages you create – you can find out how many people opened an e-mail message, clicked on a link within the message, or deleted the message without opening it.

AWeber is a good choice if you plan on creating multiple

e-mail campaigns and multiple CGI forms. It gives you an easy interface to view and manage all your campaigns at once, which can save you quite a bit of time.

At this time, there is only one package available through AWeber – you get unlimited CGI forms and unlimited autoresponder messages for $19.99 per month. You can subscribe to this service at **www.aweber.com**.

GetResponse

GetResponse offers all the same features and tools as AWeber – you can easily create CGI forms, create and configure autoresponder messages, and manage your e-mail marketing campaigns via an intuitive interface. The main difference is pricing for a large volume of subscribers – both providers charge additional monthly fees if you have more than 10,000 subscribers to your e-mail marketing lists. Although the package offered by GetResponse is slightly more expensive than AWeber's package at $22.95 per month, AWeber charges an additional $9.95 per month if you have more than 10,000 subscribers, while GetResponse charges an additional $4.95 per month.

Any Internet marketer would agree that a list of10,000 subscribers is very impressive and takes a long time to build. However, if you plan to build a very large marketing list, GetResponse might be a good solution for you.

Visitor Tracking Software

If you want your Web site to be a success and generate a substantial portion of your leads from online sources, you will need to have a means to determine how well your Web site is performing. There are a number of tools you can use to analyze the traffic on your Web site so that you can predict your site's success and make modifications to your Web site to increase its performance. Here are some of the tools that are available for tracking the traffic on your site.

StatCounter

StatCounter is a free tool you can use to analyze the traffic on your Web site and learn how you can improve your Web site's content to generate additional traffic. You can register for a free account at **www.statcounter.com**. The registration process takes just a few minutes – you will enter your contact information and a few details about your Web site, and you will have access to several features that can help you determine the success of your site.

Once you have registered your account, StatCounter will generate a block of HTML code that you can insert into each page of your Web site. This code will report information about the visitors that view your site, and you can view this information from the dashboard provided for your account on **www.statcounter.com**.

It is important that you insert the code into every page on your site, because StatCounter will not be able to access and compile information on Web pages that do not contain the code. This will cause you to miss valuable opportunities to analyze pages that might be underperforming or capitalize on pages that are performing very well.

Here are some of the statistics and information you can view from your StatCounter dashboard:

- *Popular Pages.* This feature will show you the pages of your Web site that are receiving the highest amount of visitor traffic. Ideally, your home page should receive the most traffic of any page of your Web site because you want visitors to see this page first. If another page on your site is receiving more traffic than your home page, you should analyze that page to see if it contains higher keyword density or has more inbound links than your home page.

   You can also use the Popular Pages feature to determine which pages should contain CGI forms. You can capitalize on frequently visited pages to build your e-mail marketing lists and generate more robust sales by taking advantage of the traffic flow on these pages.

- *Entry and Exit Pages.* This feature will tell you the first page visitors see when they arrive at your Web site and the last page they view before they leave your site. This will tell you which page is the most common entry point for your Web site visitors and give you an idea of how visitors navigate your Web site. If a Web page other than your contact page is the most common exit point, you might want to analyze that page to see if the content is confusing or if it contains content that is not appealing to your Web site visitors.

- *Came From.* StatCounter offers this feature to help

you determine where visitors to your site have been immediately before navigating to your site. This will tell you how many people find your site via a search engine and which search engine they are using. It will also tell you how well the inbound links that you or another Web site owner have placed on another Web site are performing – if an inbound link is performing very well, you might want to consider ways to generate more traffic for the Web page containing that link so you can drive even more traffic to your Web site.

- *Keyword Analysis.* This tool tells you what keywords search engine users are using to find pages on your Web site. A keyword that generates a high volume of traffic is a good tool for your Web site, and you can capitalize on this by increasing the keyword density of that word or phrase in your Web site content.

  If you have targeted a keyword in your content that is generating very little traffic for your Web site, it might mean that very few visitors are searching for that word or phrase or that there is a high volume of other Web sites using the same keywords. You might want to target a different keyword in your content or try increasing the density of that keyword in your content to see if its performance improves.

- *Visit Length.* This feature tells you how long visitors stay on each page of your Web site. If a page on your site has a long average visit length, it is a good indication that visitors are very interested in the content contained on that page. This is a good page to use to promote your services or build your e-mail marketing list.

If a particular page has a short average visit length, it could mean that visitors to that Web page find the material on that page confusing, or they might not consider the content relevant to their needs. It is a good idea to analyze that page to see if the content needs to be improved. If the page is not relevant to your visitors' needs and interests, you might want to consider deleting the page.

- *Returning Visitors.* This tool will tell you how many visitors have returned to each page on your site. If your home page has a high number of repeat visitors, it means that your Web site content is effective and visitors are interested in your services. If another page has many repeat visitors, you will know that the content on that Web page is very strong and that visitors are likely bookmarking that page in their favorites lists.

  If you are using e-mail marketing to build your business, use a page with frequent repeat visitors to build your subscriber base by placing a CGI form on that page.

- *Country, State, City, ISP.* StatCounter offers this feature to tell you where your visitors live or work. If you find that a high percentage of visitors live in a geographic area other than the one you service, then you might want to consider submitting your Web site to a local search engine that serves that area.

It might be that people in certain geographic areas are particularly interested in personal chef service, and this Statcounter feature gives you the ability to identify and control the flow of traffic from specific geographic areas.

When used in combination, these tools can provide a wealth of information that you can use to fine tune your online presence.

OneStatFree

Another free Web site traffic analysis tool is available at **www.onestatfree.com**. Like StatCounter, OneStatFree offers quick registration and a simple HTML block to place within your Web pages. It also offers most of the same analysis tools as StatCounter, but it includes a couple of extra tools that might be useful when you are analyzing your Web site's traffic:

- *Time Analysis.* OeStatFree offers a feature that can tell you which hours of the day, which days of the week, which weeks of the month, and which months each page receives the most traffic. While the time of day when most visitors view your site might not be important to you unless you plan to run a very limited sale on initial personal chef packages, knowing which days and months your Web pages receive the most traffic can be useful for timing autoresponder messages and announcing sales and promotions. You can also adjust your overall pricing structure to charge discounted prices during slow months, which will help you attract new clients.

- *Web Site Comparison.* OneStatFree divides registered Web sites into numerous categories, such as Arts, Business, Health and Fitness, and Weblogs. You can use the comparison tool to see how well your Web site fares in search engine rankings and other statistics, as compared to other sites in your chosen category.

  This can be a particularly useful tool for improving your Web site's content because you can easily identify Web sites that are performing better than yours. Then, you can visit those sites to analyze their content so you can gather ideas for improving the content of your own Web site.

  OneStatFree features a chart on its home page that lists all the Web site categories available – visitors of **www.onestatfree.com** can view the rankings for each category, regardless of whether they have registered accounts. This can help drive traffic to your Web site because each of the rankings contains links to the sites that are being compared.

Whether you use StatCounter or OneStatFree is a matter of personal preference. As noted in this section, OneStatFree offers additional tools for analyzing your Web site's traffic and performance, but this site is also more heavily focused on promoting its premium products, such as OneStat Web Site Analytics ($125), which provides an even greater level of detailed site analysis, and RankStat SEO Tools ($191), which assists Web site owners with tailoring content to improve search engine rankings.

There are also a number of paid visitor tracking tools

available, such as those offered at **www.metasun. com**, which can track additional statistics such as sales conversion percentages, number of file downloads, and specific visitor demographics. If you want to obtain a large amount of information about your visitors and their activities on your Web site, you can purchase Metatracker for $50 for one Web site or $125 for up to five Web sites.

Accounting, Business, and Financial Tools

As you have learned throughout this book, establishing and running a personal chef business takes more than just the ability to craft fine, tasty cuisine – it also takes a high level of business savvy. There are several tools available that can help you manage the business side of your venture and make your business more profitable.

Accounting and Financial Tools

One of the crucial elements of building a successful personal chef business is the ability to effectively manage your business' money. Profitable businesses have to account for marketing, inventory, material, and other expenses, while pricing products to provide revenue over and above these expenses.

These tools can help you manage your business' finances so you can reduce expenses and maximize profit.

Microsoft Money

Microsoft Money is a software application that can help you manage and track your finances all in one place. You can purchase Microsoft Money Plus Home and Business at **www.microsoft.com/money/default.mspx** for $89.99; however, Microsoft frequently offers a $30 mail in rebate, so you can obtain this software for a final price of $59.99. You can also download a free 60-day trial of this software from the same Web site so you can familiarize yourself with the features before you purchase it.

Microsoft Money Plus Home and Business gives you basic features available in many software packages, such as checkbook balancing, spending categorization, and budget creation. It also allows you to prepare for tax season and manage your investments, such as IRA contributions, stocks, and money market accounts.

You can also download transactions from most major financial institutions to Microsoft Money Home and Business so you will not have to manually update your accounts when you log in to the software program.

It also gives you a number of business tools to help you manage your business, such as invoice creation, compilation of business reports, payroll management, and invoice and receivables monitoring.

Quicken

Quicken is another financial management software tool that you can use to make sure your business stays profitable. At $59.99, it is somewhat less expensive than Microsoft Money Home and Business, although it lacks a number of the business features of Microsoft Money.

Specifically, the current version of Quicken does not give

you the ability to create business reports or invoices, and does not allow you to manage payroll tasks online. If these functions are not important to you, Quicken will easily handle most of the other elements required to keep your creative business financially sound.

You can purchase Quicken 2008 at **http://quicken.intuit. com**; however, the Web site does not currently offer a free trial version of the software, so you will not be able to test its features before you make a purchase.

GnuCash

GnuCash is a free alternative to Microsoft Money Home and Business and Quicken. When you download the software from **www.gnucash.org**, you will have access to a number of tools that will allow you to effectively manage your personal and business finances.

GnuCash allows you to set up multiple accounts so you can manage your personal checking, savings, business, and investment accounts from one dashboard. You can also set up accounts payable to manage your expenditures for supplies and marketing expenses, liability accounts to handle your personal and business loans, and credit card accounts to keep track of your unsecured debt. You can also use GnuCash to manage payroll tasks, create customer invoices, manage customer and vendor data, and keep track of tax and billing terms for your customers.

This software application features frequent updates, so you will not have to worry about your software becoming obsolete. Like Microsoft Money Home and Business and

Quicken, GnuCash even gives you the ability to download transactions from the Web sites of major financial institutions, so updating your accounts is an effortless process.

With a variety of functions and features, GnuCash can be an excellent financial management solution if you do not want to invest your money in a paid financial software package.

Business Tools

You can also use tools that will help you create a business plan. Creating a business plan can seem like a daunting task if you have never undertaken the endeavor of creating one for a business. Fortunately, you can access resources that will provide you with sample plans for a variety of business types and give you templates that you can use to create your own business plan.

BPlans

You can access over 500 sample business plans at **www. bplans.com**. These plans represent a wide variety of business plan styles and provide samples of plans for various industries. Viewing sample business plans can be a great exercise before you create your own plan – you get to see how different businesses approach their plans and identify techniques that will be effective in your own business plan.

This Web site also contains many articles that cover different aspects of your plan, giving you advice about what types of information to include and how to present the information so that your business vision will be communicated clearly and effectively to potential investors, loan officers, and other people who will have the power to influence the success of your business and help you reach your financial and career goals.

You can also access several calculators that will help you create a realistic roadmap for your business – you can use these tools to calculate startup costs, determine when your business will break even, and even determine the return on investment you can expect from paid advertising efforts, such as pay-per-click marketing.

Business Plan Pro

If you need additional assistance to create a business plan, you might consider purchasing Business Plan Pro. This software includes over 500 business plan samples and gives you a number of templates to build your own plan. Using this software gives you step-by-step assistance in creating a business plan, so you can make sure that all elements of your business are considered and included in your final business plan document.

You can also import data from Excel spreadsheets or Quicken to streamline the financial analysis portion of the plan. This feature will save you hours of time that you would otherwise spend transferring numbers and statistics from another document to your business plan.

Business Plan Pro is available at **www.bplans.com/mk/ bpp_jp.cfm** for $99.95.

The tools described in this chapter can be invaluable in getting your creative business started and achieving success once your business is up and running.

Case Studies

CASE STUDY: ALLISON J. COIA

Allison J. Coia

Owner/Chef

Cook A Doodle Doo Personal Chef Service

After 911, I was furloughed for a corporate job and was searching for a new career. I came across this industry after conducting some internet searches. I stumbled upon Personal Chefs Network and I have not looked back since.

I was raised in an Italian kitchen, growing up with a parent who was the "queen" of the family cooks. She had a keen eye for new and innovative ideas and through my careful watching and helping, it caught on. We owned a deli and catering business growing up, so being around food was a constant. I also dabbled in cooking for a food service company after high school, but decided I wanted to work a "normal" job.

I serve three to four clients on a weekly basis. These clients mostly consist of monthly clients, along with a few bi-weekly clients. On open days, I try to fill with one-time gigs, like a personal chef gift certificate.

CASE STUDY: ALLISON J. COIA

Being featured in newspapers and local magazine articles has been a great confidence booster and a wonderful marketing tool. I also have had the pleasure of cooking for a Philadelphia 76er basketball player. This experience has been great exposure for me. His involvement in the community is inspiring and right up my alley, since I love others who can spread their kindness.

I love my schedule. I use Mondays as my planning/office day and specialty shopping day. I only cook Tuesdays through Fridays, and I am done my work day by 5 p.m. like everyone else. Since I have an established personal chef business, I no longer offer a party service. There are no nights and weekends for me. Also, the people I have had the opportunity to meet have been awesome. The worst part is the isolation that this job can bring. There are days I do not see any clients and my only interaction are the people at the grocery store.

Be willing to put yourself out there. The cooking part is easy, but like any other business, you need to market and be very diligent about it. Just because I am established does not mean I can stop marketing and getting my name out in public. I also suggest joining a reputable organization. I have found that being "certified" by some organizations is unnecessary. It is not required in any state and in over six years of business, I have never been asked for it.

CASE STUDY: CHEF DARNELL HARNESS

Chef Darnell Harness

Owner, SimplyDine Personal Chef Service

chefdarnell@cox.net

702-768-0010

I wanted to help people who were not able to cook quality food, especially the elderly. I also wanted to prepare food for those who have health challenges, such as diabetes and heart disease.

My background is in the medical profession as a Sonographer. After I decided to venture into the culinary field, I enrolled in UNLV's Professional Chef Certification Program, through Creative Cooking School.

Generally, clients do not request many changes to my menu items. The reason for this is that I ask my clients to complete a very comprehensive questionnaire before I start preparing their menus and cooking for them. The questionnaire covers their personal preferences, dietary restrictions, allergies, and so on.

I like being able to provide people with more time, quality food, choices on when and where to eat, and how they like their food prepared. It is very rewarding to see my clients enjoy their food. I do not appreciate it when people do not see the value of a personal chef service and haggle on the price of services. I think there is a big misperception that either personal chefs are only for the rich or that personal chefs should be paid the same as fast food workers.

If you are just starting out in the personal chef business, be patient, do plenty of advertising, and continue to learn and hone your skills as a chef. Try to align yourself with as many good organizations as possible, such as the Celiac Foundation, the Diabetes Foundation, and the American Heart Association. Go to different stores and do cooking demos — these are good advertising opportunities. Ask some of the culinary arts schools whether they need teachers.

CASE STUDY: DOUG JANOUSEK

Doug Janousek

Home Cookin' LLC

706-410-0541

After 25 years as a working journalist, and a lifetime of cooking and traveling all around the United States as well as writing about food, I attended culinary school at the Orlando Culinary Academy where I received my AAS and my Le Cordon Bleu certification. I graduated in December 2005 and officially launched my personal chef business in January 2006.

I started my personal chef business so that I could have the immediate satisfaction of cooking for clients rather than work in a large kitchen and never see the folks who eat my food. I enjoy the more intimate setting of cooking for individual clients.

Initially, when I launched my business in 2006 it took about three months of daily marketing and public relations efforts to attract my first clients. After relocating to Georgia, I had my first cooking gigs within a week or two of physically relocating, though to be honest, I had done a fair amount of advance publicity before the move.

One of the greatest successes I have experienced as a personal chef was when I was hired to prepare an authentic Austrian meal at the Austrian Consulate in Orlando, it was a great honor and a fun challenge. Another great achievement was when I published my first cookbook with other personal chefs. I am now working on a second cookbook that will feature Georgia artists and my menus and recipes. I am also working on a high-end chef's tasting menu event with a local restaurant as a way to create "buzz" and make a little money.

If I had to start my personal chef business over again, I would evaluate advertising differently. I allowed myself to be talked into certain kinds of

CASE STUDY: DOUG JANOUSEK

advertising that in the end cost a lot of money and did not pay off – to be exact, I found Yellow Pages advertising to be the least effective. Online, targeted newspaper ads and publicity events have worked the best for me.

CASE STUDY: CHEF KIMBERLY OROPEZA

Chef Kimberly Oropeza

A Taste of Thyme Cheffing Services

407-341-9234

www.atasteofthyme.net

I started my personal chef business because I was looking for something that I could do to make some extra money and have a flexible schedule. I had heard about personal chefs and at that time I was becoming more and more interested in cooking. Finally my family convinced me that I should give it a try.

The number of clients I serve varies based on the season and my schedule. When I am working my business part-time I usually have one or two per week. When I am working full-time I may have four.

It took just a few weeks to find my first client. When I first started as a personal chef, I joined the Personal Chefs Network, which posts your information

CASE STUDY: CHEF KIMBERLY OROPEZA

on their Web site. That is where my first client found me. Now, I receive numerous referrals from existing clients, and many of those referrals hire me as their personal chef.

I have had a number of great moments as a personal chef. In addition to the personal chef service, I added catering services to my business a few years ago. Each large event that I have catered has been a success. When a bride or a party's host tells you that they loved everything, it is a great feeling. Other milestones include personal chef and catering services for well-known people or companies. I have catered a dinner party for winners of a Real Simple magazine contest, and I have provided chef services for a well-known musical group, as well as a professional basketball player.

Being independent is the aspect of being a personal chef that I like most; however, it is also the aspect that I sometimes like the least. I generally like to work on my own and being a personal chef gives me that opportunity. However, there are times when I need a gentle push to get things done, or someone to get advice from, and I don't have that.

If you enjoy cooking, and you think you might like to try a career as a personal chef, just go for it. It does not take a lot of training, and it takes very little investment to get started. Just a set of pans, some kitchen utensils, and some pantry items and you are good to go. You can always try it on the side and build up business if you are not ready to jump in full force.

Bibliography

Vivaldo, Denise. *How to Start a Home Based Personal Chef Business*, 1st Ed. Guilford, CT: Globe Pequot, 2006

Wallace, Candy. *The Professional Personal Chef: The Business of Doing Business as a Personal Chef*. Hoboken, NJ: John Wiley and Sons, Inc., 2008

Bilderback, Leslie. *The Complete Idiot's Guide to Success as a Chef*. New York, NY: Penguin Group, 2006

The Culinary Institute of America, *The Professional Chef*. New York, NY: John Wiley and Sons, Inc., 2002

Dedication & Biography

This book is dedicated to the late Elric Morningstar, who inspired and encouraged us to follow our passions and to listen to the still, small voices inside of us, even when we think those voices are crazy.

Carla and Lee Rowley are the owners of Java Joint Media, a full-service copywriting firm based in Columbus, Ohio. When not writing, Lee and Carla are vegan chefs, constantly creating innovative, healthy dishes using fresh, organic, animal-free ingredients. To learn more about Java Joint Media, please visit **www.javajointmedia.com.** For a list of vegan recipes you can try out yourself, visit Lee's recipe blog at **http://veggieguy.blogspot.com.**

Glossary

Here, you will find some of the most commonly used terms in the personal chef industry. You will also find a number of terms related to building and promoting your business, both online and offline. Be sure to bookmark this glossary as a handy reference as your personal chef business takes flight.

Adobo sauce: A spicy sauce commonly used in Latin American and Southwest U.S. dishes. This sauce is made from chipotle peppers, garlic, cumin, onion, vinegar, and a tomato based sauce, such as catsup.

Aioli: A type of mayonnaise which originates from the province region of southern France. This type of sauce is typically flavored with garlic, and is commonly used in meat, fish, and vegetable dishes.

A la carte: In a personal chef's menu, this term means that each item is available individually, and is priced separately.

Al dente: In Italian, this term means "to the tooth." Pasta and vegetables that are cooked al dente are not soft or overdone, but rather, maintain a level of firmness. Vegetables that are current al dente are somewhat crunchy, and are not meant to be completely tender.

Amaranth: A nourishing food which is slightly sweet in flavor, and is high in protein. The amaranth seed can be used as a cereal, or may be ground into a flour for making bread.

Ancho: A fresh green poblano chili pepper which has been dried. Ancho chilis are rich in flavor, and have a slightly sweet fruit flavor. They are typically deep red or brown in color, and can either be mild or very hot.

Andouille: A type of smoked sausage frequently used in traditional Cajun cuisine. The sausage is heavily spiced, and is made from tripe and pork chitterlings. It commonly appears in jumbalaya, gumbo, and other Cajun dishes.

Anise: A spice that is made from the leaves and seed of the anise plant, a member of the parsley family. This spice has a heavy, sweet licorice flavor.

Arborio rice: A grain grown in Italy that has a high starch content. This grain is typically used for making risotto, because it creates a creamy texture as it is cooked.

Aromatic: Any of a number of spices, or plants that are used to impart flavor and fragrance to food or drinks.

Aspic: A savory jelly that has a clear or opaque appearance. This jelly is made of gelatin and clarified stock made from meat, fish, or vegetables. Aspics are typically served on cold plates so that the jelly will not melt before it is eaten.

Au jus: A food that is served with its own natural juices. This term is most commonly associated with beef; however, certain root vegetables, such as beets, may be served au jus as well.

Baba ghannouj: A Mediterranean and Middle Eastern dip made with roasted eggplants and spices. Chickpeas and tahini are sometimes added to this dish. The eggplants are typically roasted with the skins left on to impart a unique, smoky flavor – after roasting, the eggplants are mashed and the skins discarded. This dip is most commonly served with fresh or baked pita bread.

Baguette: A loaf of French bread which is long and narrow, and which exhibits a crisp brown crust and a chewy inside.

Baking powder: A powder which is used to leaven bread. When baking powder is mixed with a liquid, it releases carbon dioxide gas bubbles that allow breads and cakes to rise. It is important to keep baking powder in a cool, dry place to maximize shelf life.

Baking soda: A powder which is used to leaven cake batter or bread. When baking soda is mixed with an acid, such as butter milk or yogurt, it produces carbon dioxide gas bubbles that allow the cake batter or bread dough to rise. For this reason, it is important to mix baking soda with dry ingredients before adding butter milk or yogurt, since it reacts quickly with these ingredients.

Basil: the leaves of a basil plant, which is a member of the mint family. Basil leaves are typically green and leafy, but can also be purple in color. Basil has a pungent taste that can be described as a combination of licorice and cloves. It can be used in a variety of dishes, and is the primary ingredient in pesto.

Basmati rice: A type of rice typically used in Indian cuisine. It is a long grain rice with a fine texture and a fragrant aroma. This type of rice is typically described as having a nutty flavor. In order to reduce its moisture content, basmati rice is aged before use.

Baste: A cooking technique in which a food is continuously spooned or brushed with liquid. A variety of liquids are used in basting, such as meat or vegetable stock, wine, butter, or fat. The purpose of basting is to ensure the optimal color, flavor, and moisture of foods.

Bay leaf: The leaf of the evergreen bay laurel tree, which is used as an aromatic herb to flavor meat dishes, vegetables, stews, and soups. Although dry bay leaves are more commercially available than fresh ones, they lend less flavor to a dish. It is important to limit the number of bay leaves used in a dish because they can cause a dish to have a bitter flavor. Always remove the bay leaves from a stew, soup, or dish before serving.

Bearnaise sauce: A French sauce that is traditionally used to accompany meat, fish, vegetables, and eggs. It is made from egg yolks, wine, butter, tarragon, shallots, and a vinegar reduction.

Bechamel sauce: A French white sauce that is made by

adding milk to a roux of butter and flour. The thickness of this sauce might vary according to the proportion of the milk to the roux.

Beurre blanc: A French sauce that is used for vegetables, eggs, poultry, and seafood. It is made from wine, vinegar, and shallots. Chunks of cold butter are whisked into a reduction of these ingredients to achieve the desired thickness.

Bind: A cooking technique which is used to thicken a sauce or hot liquid by stirring in an ingredient, such as flour or dairy products.

Bisque: A soup known for its hardy, rich flavor. This soup is made from cream and pureed seafood, although sometimes poultry or vegetables are used.

Blackened: A dish prepared according to a traditional style of Cajun cooking. Typically, this consists of a cut of meat or fish which has been rubbed in Cajun spices, then cooked in a very hot cast iron skillet to allow a dark, crisp, flavorful crust to form.

Blanch: A technique used in cooking in which the fruit or vegetables are briefly immersed in boiling water, then immediately soaked in cold water to stop further cooking from occurring. This technique allows fruit and vegetables to achieve maximum color and flavor, and have a firm texture.

Boil: A cooking technique in which foods are immersed in liquid that has been brought to a temperature of 212 degrees Fahrenheit or higher.

Bolognese: A dish which consists of a thick meat and vegetable sauce with wine and cream added to intensify the flavor and increase the thickness.

Bordelaise sauce: A French sauce that is most commonly served with broiled meats. It is made from a red or white wine, bone marrow, shallots, brown stock, parsley, and various herbs.

Bouillon: Liquid which has been strained off after treat, meat, fish, or vegetables have been cooked in water. This can be used as a base for various soups and sauces.

Bouquet garni: A combination of parsley, thyme, and bay leaf. These are typically either tied together or wrapped in cheesecloth and are used to flavor broths, soups, and stews.

Braise: A cooking method in which meat or vegetables are covered in fat or liquid, then cooked in a tightly covered container with a small amount of liquid. This cooking occurs at a low heat for an extended period of time, either on the stovetop or in the oven. The purpose of braising a food is to increase its flavor and tenderness by breaking down its fibers.

Broil: A cooking technique in which a food is cooked in an oven directly under the gas or electric heat source. It can also refer to cooking food on a barbecue grill directly over the charcoal or gas heat source.

Cajun seasoning: A seasoning blend which is frequently used in Cajun cooking to impart a bold taste. Cajun seasoning is made from black pepper, mustard, chili peppers, celery, onion, and garlic. Some versions of the seasoning also include cayenne pepper.

Caraway seed: A seed that comes from the parsley family and is known for its aromatic qualities and nutty flavor. This seed can be used in savory and sweet cooking.

Cardamom: a spice that is a member of the ginger family and consists of a seed contained within a pod. This aromatic spice can be used whole or ground, or only the seed may be used. It has a spicy, sweet flavor, and is very pungent.

Cayenne pepper: A spice that is made from various tropical chili peppers, including the hot Cayenne pepper. In some stores, this may also be called red pepper.

Cheesecloth: A type of thin cloth made from fine or coarse woven cotton that is used for straining liquids. Cheesecloth can also be used as bags for herbs and spices used to flavor dishes when the herbs must be removed before the dish is served.

Chiffonade: Herbs or vegetables that are either sliced or shredded and used as garnish for soups and other dishes. The herbs and vegetables may be used raw, or they may be lightly cooked.

Chili powder: A blend of herbs and spices used to lend spiciness and flavor, usually to a tomato based dish. Chili powder is made from dried chili peppers, garlic, cloves, oregano, coriander, and cumin.

Chinois: A sieve used for straining and pureeing. Usually made of metal, a chinois has mesh that is very fine, so a ladle or other tool must be used to press ingredients through it.

Chipotle: A chipotle is not a separate kind of pepper; rather, it is a jalapeno that has been smoked and dried. These peppers are commonly used in Mexican sauces and certain types of stews to lend a spicy, slightly sweet flavor to the dish. You might find chipotles dried, canned in adobo sauce, or pickled.

Chive: An herb that is related to the onion. This fragrant herb has a thin green stem that is hollow and has a mild onion flavor. It is typically used fresh rather than dried, and is usually added to a dish at the end of cooking to preserve its flavor.

Choron sauce: A French sauce in which tomato puree is added to a classic hollandaise or béarnaise sauce. Choron sauce is usually served with meat dishes, such as poultry or fish, although it is occasionally used with beef dishes as well.

Chutney: A sweet, spicy sauce that is typically served with Indian dishes to provide a contrast to the pungent aroma and strong flavor of these foods. To make a chutney, fruits such as mangos are mixed with sugar, spices, and vinegar.

Cilantro: The green leaf and stem of the coriander plant. This herb is typically used in spicy Mexican dishes to impart a fresh, bold flavor. You may find this in stores as cilantro, coriander, or Chinese parsley.

Clarified butter: Also called ghee, this butter is slowly melted via a low heat source. As the unsalted butter is melted, the milk solids separate and the golden liquid that forms at the top is removed and used in cooking. Clarified butter is commonly used in Indian dishes.

Clove: An unopened flower bud of the tropical evergreen clove tree. This spice has a pungent aroma and unique flavor that adds depth to Indian dishes and other food. You can find cloves whole or ground. If you are using ground cloves, keep in mind that this spice typically has a shelf life of six months or less – after that, it begins to lose its aroma and flavor.

Compound butter: Butter that is softened and mixed with garlic, chives, parsley, or wine. You can cook with compound butter, but it is most commonly used as a spread or filling.

Confit: A dish made of meat that is preserved and then cooked in its own fat. Duck and goose are the types of meat most commonly used in confit dishes, although other types of meats may also be used.

Consomme: The broth or stock of meat or fish, which has been clarified by cooking. Consomme is often served as a hot or cold soup, but it can also be used as the base for a sauce or soup.

Coriander: Another name for cilantro. This herb is the green leaf and stem of the coriander plant. The seeds of this plant may also be used in cooking to add a complex taste and unique aroma.

Cornstarch: A starch that is commonly used to thicken

sauces and dishes such as soups or puddings. Cornstarch can also be used with grains to achieve a more elastic consistency – some pizza dough recipes call for cornstarch. It is typically mixed with a small amount of water before being added to a dish to prevent clumping.

Coulis: A thick paste or sauce used in a variety of dishes. Tomatoes and red bell peppers are commonly used to make coulis.

Cream Sauce: A French béchamel sauce that is made with milk or cream. It is occasionally served alone as a compliment to another dish, but may also be used in the preparation of a dish to add a rich texture and flavor.

Cremini: A small brown mushroom that is related to the portobello. These mushrooms are often used in Italian dishes, although they may also be used in Asian dishes or served with garlic butter.

Cumin: The dried fruit of a plant from the parsley family. Cumin has an earthy, nutty taste and a distinctive aroma. You will typically find cumin ground, although whole seeds can be purchased for use with certain dishes. Cumin is commonly used in Indian curry dishes, and is also used in chili powder.

Curry: A hot, spicy blend that is used in many Indian dishes. There are many spices used in curry, including cardamom, cloves, chili peppers, cumin, nutmeg, and red and black pepper. Sesame seeds, saffron, and turmeric are also often used in this spice blend. Curry may also refer to an Indian dish that uses this spice blend.

Deglaze: A cooking technique in which liquid is added to a pan over heat to loosen browned bits left over from browning meats and fish. This liquid is commonly used as a stock, and can be made into a sauce to accompany the meat or fish that was previously cooked in the same pan.

Degrease: The technique of using a spoon to skim layers of fat or grease from the top of a cooked liquid. This technique is commonly used with soups, gravy, sauces, and soup stock.

Dill: A green herb with feathery leaves that resemble pine needles. Dill is typically used fresh rather than dried or ground, and imparts a pungent flavor and aroma to a variety of foods. Dill seeds may also be used in cooking to add an even stronger taste.

Emulsifier: An ingredient which is used to bind two liquids that cannot otherwise be combined, such as wines and oils. An emulsifier can also be used to thicken soups and sauces.

Emulsion: A cooking mixture that contains two liquids that cannot be combined without the aid of an emulsifier. Eggs are commonly used in emulsions to bind the two liquids together.

Felafel: A Middle Eastern dish consisting of ground chickpeas mixed with olive oil and spices. This mixture is formed into golf ball sized pieces and deep fried. Felafel may be served alone as an appetizer, or as a filling in pita bread with fresh lettuce, tomatos, onions, and tahini. Felafel is a common staple of vegetarian and vegan cooking, because

How to Open & Operate a Financially Successful Personal Chef Business

the chickpeas provide protein that would otherwise be provided by meat dishes.

Fennel: An aromatic plant that imparts a licorice flavor to various dishes. It can be found whole or ground as a spice.

Five-spice: A mixture of spices commonly used in Chinese dishes. Five-spice powder is made from ground cinnamon, cloves, fennel seed, star anise, and peppercorns.

Flax: a high protein food commonly added to a vegetarian and vegan dishes. Flax seeds are high in omega 3 fatty acids, which can be difficult to obtain in vegetarian and vegan diets. Flax seeds may be added to pasta dishes, or may be ground into flour for making bread. Also, flax seed oil may be used to add flavor and nutrients to meatless dishes.

Fumet: A stock made from fish or mushrooms. This stock is concentrated, and can be used to add flavor to other stocks and sauces.

Garam Masala: A spice blend that is commonly used in Indian dishes. It consists of cinnamon, cloves, black pepper, cardamom, cumin, coriander, dried chili peppers, nutmeg, and other spices. This blend imparts a pungent aroma and distinctive taste to vegetable based Indian dishes.

Ghee: Another term for clarified butter, which is made by slowly cooking unsalted butter over a low heat to remove the milk solids. The remaining golden liquid is used in many Indian dishes.

Ginger: A spice made from the ginger root, which is used to add a spicy flavor to Indian, Chinese, African, and Jamaican dishes. You can find ginger in many forms – it can be grated from fresh ginger root, dried and ground, pickled, or candied. Pickled ginger is also used as an accompaniment to sushi dishes, to provide a contrast to the taste of the rice and fish.

Glaze: A thin sauce that is used to coat various foods. A glaze gives meats and vegetables a shiny, smooth texture and look, and can impart sweet or spicy flavors to foods.

Gravy: A sauce that is usually made with milk, wine, or broth – any of these ingredients can be combined with meat or vegetable juices to make a gravy. Gravies can also be thickened with flour or cornstarch. They may be served as an accompaniment to meat or potato dishes, or may be added to these foods at the end of preparation and just before serving.

Herbes de province: An herb blend originating from southern France that is used to enhance the flavor of meat and vegetable dishes. Herbes de province is made with basil, rosemary, sage, thyme, lavender, fennel seed, and other herbs. It can be purchased as a ready made mixture or can be made with freshly dried individual herbs.

Hollandaise sauce: A sauce that is made from butter, egg yolks, and lemon juice. This creamy sauce can be served with eggs Benedict, or with other dishes, such as fish and vegetables.

Hummus: A Middle Eastern dip made from cooked, pureed chickpeas, garlic, cumin, tahini, and lemon juice. Other ingredients such as roasted red bell peppers, black pepper, jalapenos, or crushed red pepper can be added to hummus to create unique flavors. This dip is commonly served with fresh vegetables or pita bread, but it can also be used in wraps, gyros, and falafel dishes.

Jasmine rice: A long grain rice with a fragrant aroma that is often used in Thai dishes.

Jerk seasoning: A spice blend used in Jamaican dishes. It is made from chili peppers, thyme, cinnamon, ginger, allspice, onion, garlic, and cloves. It can either be used as a marinade, or as a rub to season grilled meats, such as chicken and fish.

Leek: A vegetable with a soft onion flavor that is commonly used in soups and salads. The leek is related to garlic and the onion.

Lemongrass: A fragrant herb with a pungent lemon flavor that is frequently used in Thai dishes. You can find lemongrass in fresh and dried form – fresh lemongrass imparts a much stronger flavor to foods.

Louis sauce: A sauce that can be used to accompany seafood dishes. It is made from mayonnaise, chili sauce, scallions, lemon juice, green peppers, cream, and spices.

Lyonnaise sauce: A French sauce that is made from white wine, onions, and demi glaze. This sauce is typically served with meat dishes.

Maltaise sauce: A sauce that uses hollandaise sauce with orange juice and orange zest added. It can be served as an accompaniment to cooked green vegetables, like asparagus and green beans.

Marinade: Any of a variety of liquids that is used to add flavor to a meat, vegetable, or meat substitute dish. Marinades are typically made from lemon juice, vinegar, or wine with herbs and spices added. Foods such as meats, vegetables, and tofu can be soaked in marinades for several hours to add a strong flavor and aroma. The taste imparted by the marinade varies according to the types of herbs and spices used.

Marinara: A tomato sauce used in classic Italian dishes which contains garlic, oregano, and onions. Marinara can be used in pasta, vegetable, and meat dishes.

Marjoram: A mint like herb that has a flavor that is similar to oregano. It is typically used in vegetable and meat dishes, particularly those containing veal or lamb. Because marjoram has a light flavor, it is typically added to dishes at the end of the cooking process. You can purchase marjoram in either fresh or dried form.

Matzo: A bread made from plain white flour and water, which forms a cracker like food commonly used in Jewish cuisine, particularly during Passover when leavened breads are forbidden. It can also be crumbled and used to form matzo balls, or added to fish and other dishes to bind ingredients together.

Medallion: Meat or vegetables that are cut into coin shapes.

Mirepoix: A flavoring agent used in stocks, sauces, soups, stews, and gravies. It is made from onions, celery, and carrots. The ratio of these ingredients varies according to the type of dish that the mirepoix will be used in.

Monosodium glutamate: A powder made of 22 amino acids that is used to enhance to flavor of food. It is typically used in Japanese and Chinese dishes. Many people have adverse physical reactions to MSG, so it is a good idea to omit this ingredient whenever possible. If it is not possible to eliminate MSG from a particular dish, let your clients know that the meal contains this ingredient.

Mornay sauce: A béchamel sauce that contains parmesan or Swiss cheese. This sauce is served with chicken, vegetable, fish, and egg dishes. Some chefs add cream, egg yolks, or chicken stock to this sauce to enhance its flavor.

Mustard: Liquid or powder derived from seeds of the mustard plant that is used to flavor meats, vegetables, and salad dressings. Mustard can also be used as an ingredient in spice blends and rubs.

Nutmeg: A spice with a sweet, pungent taste and aroma. It is commonly used in potato and vegetable dishes, and can also be used in custards and other desserts.

Oregano: A mint herb that resembles marjoram, but with a stronger aroma and taste. Oregano is frequently used in tomato sauces and pasta dishes, and can be purchased fresh or dried and ground.

Organic: Foods that are grown without the use of chemicals, synthetic fertilizers, or insecticides. Organic foods are typically more expensive than conventionally grown foods, but some people will be willing to pay more for meals that contain organic ingredients because of the perceived increased health benefits.

Panko: Coarse bread crumbs used to coat foods to give them a crunchy texture. Panko is typically used in Japanese fried dishes.

Parsley: A green, leafy herb that comes both fresh and dried. Parsley has a hint of a peppery taste and can be used for seasoning and as an attractive garnish.

Peppercorn: This spice is used to accent the flavor of both sweet and savory foods. The three main types of peppercorns are black, green, and white. It can be purchased whole, cracked, coarsely ground, and finely ground. Whole peppercorns carry the most flavor.

Pepperoncini: A sweet, mild pepper that has a slight heat to it. Peperoncini are normally packaged and sold by the jar. They can be used as garnishes and on salads and sandwiches.

Pesto: An uncooked, pureed sauce that is typically made up of basil, garlic, pine nuts, Parmesan cheese, and olive oil. It can be used as a spread on Italian breads or over pasta.

Pilaf: A rice dish that is browned with oil and cooked in seasoned broth. Vegetables and meats can be added to rice pilaf to suit the preference of the person it is prepared for.

Poach: A cooking method that adds tenderness and flavor to foods. Meats, vegetables, and fruits can be cooked in liquid just below boiling, allowing the food being poached to soak up the flavor of the liquid.

Poblano Chili Pepper: The type of pepper most often used in chili rellano. These peppers can range from mild to hot in flavor. The color of the pepper helps to identify the richness of the pepper. The darker the pepper, the richer the flavor will be. There is also a dry form known as the ancho chili.

Polenta: A dish made from boiled cornmeal. It can be eaten either hot or cold and sometimes mixed with Parmesan and other cheeses to add flavor.

Portabello: A large mushroom that can be used as a meat replacement. Portabellos can be seasoned and grilled to be used on sandwiches. They can also be oven roasted and sauteed.

Puree: Food that has been ground or crushed into a paste or thick liquid.

Ragu: A sauce made of ground beef, tomatoes, onion, celery, carrots, white wine, and seasonings. This sauce is served over pasta.

Ratatouille: A French dish that is made up of tomatoes, eggplant, bell peppers, zuchinni, onion, garlic, and herbs cooked in olive oil. Ratatouille can be eaten either hot or cold and can be a main or side dish.

Red pepper flakes: Different types of hot red chili peppers that are ground into red pepper.

Reduce: To boil a liquid until it begins to thicken into a thicker sauce. This process creates a more potent flavor.

Remoulade: A French sauce made up primarily of mayonnaise mixed with mustard, capers, chopped gherkins, anchovies, and herbs. This sauce is served chilled with seafoods and meats.

Render: The process of cooking meat at low or medium heat to melt the fat and allowing it to be separated from the meat.

Roast: To cook food uncovered in the oven. This method of cooking is commonly used for tender meats and vegetables. Food will cook to a dark color on the outside, but the center will remain moist.

Rosemary: A common herb that comes fresh, dried, or powdered. It is best used for seasoning food with strong flavors.

Roulade: A thin slice of meat rolled around a filling of cheese, vegetables, or other meat. It is normally browned on the stove before being baked or braised in wine.

Roux: Used most often in French cooking, it is a mixture of wheat, flour, and fat. It can be used as a base for gravy and sauces.

Saffron: A bitter tasting spice that comes from the flower of saffron crocus.

Sage: A slightly bitter tasting herb that comes fresh, dried, or ground. It can be used in some pasta and meat dishes.

Samosas: Triangular pastries stuffed with potatoes, green peas, onions, and spices, then deep fried. Samosas are common appetizers in Indian cuisine, and can be served alone or with a chutney for dipping.

Saute: To cook on high heat, to speed cooking, in a small amount of fat.

Scallion: More commonly known as green onions. They can be served fresh and whole with a variety of foods and also make an attractive garnish.

Sear: A method of using very high heat, such as a broiler or hot oven, to lock the moisture before cooking takes place.

Seitan: A common meat replacement used in vegetarian cooking. It can be prepared in many different ways to offer a variety of flavor.

Serrano: A type of chili pepper that is very meaty and does not dry well. They typically come in red, brown, orange, and yellow.

Sesame seed: Seeds that add a nutty taste to dishes they are used in. They are commonly used in Asian dishes.

Shallot: A relative to the onion, but with a sweeter, milder flavor.

Simmer: Cooking foods in liquid just below boiling. If the liquid is at the correct temperature, tiny bubbles will begin to break the surface of the liquid.

Skim: A method used to remove the top layer of fat from foods such as stocks, soups, milk, and creams.

Star anise: A dark brown, star-shaped spice that has a bitter taste.

Steam: A method of cooking with a steamer to keep the foods original taste, shape, and texture.

Stock: A simmered mixture of meats or vegetables that is used as a base for soups, stews, and sauces.

Sweat: This method allows vegetables and herbs to cook in their own juices over low heat until they are aromatic.

Tahini: A paste made from ground sesame seeds. This paste is commonly used in hummus or as a spread for gyros or falafel dishes.

Tapas: A variety of Spanish appetizers that can be cold, such as olives and cheese, or warm, such as fried baby squid or puntillitas. It is frequently served with red wine or sherry.

Tapenade: A popular French hors d'oeuvre. A dish made up of pureed or finely chopped olives, capers, and olive oil.

Tarragon: A French herb that has a similar flavor to anise.

Tempeh: Commonly used in vegetarian and vegan cooking. Tempeh is soybean made into a thin cake by cooking the soybeans and using a method of controlled fermentation to mold them into a thin, white cake.

Thyme: A common herb that comes in fresh, powdered, or

dried form. It is used in a variety of dishes and blends well with other herbs without overpowering them.

Tofu: Also known as bean curd, tofu is a common meat substitute used in vegetarian and vegan cooking. Tofu has very little flavor by itself, but can be seasoned and marinated to take on more flavor.

Truffle: A variety of fungi. They come in many different forms and can be used in sauces, pastas, and omelets.

Turmeric: An herb that is ground into an orange-yellow powder. It has a bitter, peppery flavor and smells like mustard.

Veloute sauce: A white sauce that is stock based and thickened with white roux.

Vinaigrette: Typically used as a salad dressing, it is a basic oil and vinegar combination.

Zest: The outer, colorful skin of a citrus fruit. It can be used to add flavor to lemon meringue pie, sorbets, and salads.

Index

Symbols

401K 197, 198

A

Advertising 184, 185
Alternative 136, 137
Analysis 57, 58, 60
Applicants 114, 118, 119, 122, 125

B

Browser 233, 235
Budget 83- 89
Business card 202

C

Candidate 114-116, 118, 121, 122, 125
Capital 46, 50, 64, 69, 70, 72-74, 78, 80
Captial 84
Career 13-15, 19, 20, 21, 25
Cater 22, 29, 36, 71, 76, 152
Cholesterol 134-138
Clean 91, 94, 97, 98
Client 15, 22-31, 86, 91, 94, 96-98,
        100-109, 132-143, 156, 158,
        160-163, 168-170, 173-180,
        183-185, 189, 190, 201, 213, 261,
        262
Comment Cards 156, 157, 163, 165,
        170, 171, 174, 175
Competition 51, 53, 56, 57, 70, 73, 77,
        181, 182, 187, 188

Complaint 155, 172
Condition 104
Contact 156, 161, 168, 177, 178
Content 210-212, 214-217, 219, 221,
        222, 224-227, 230, 244-247, 249
Contract 117, 126, 128, 130, 163, 168,
        176, 179
Conversation 157, 166, 168, 174, 177
Cook 14, 16, 22, 25, 27-30, 32, 35, 36,
        88, 93, 98
Credentials 186
Culinary 33-37, 41, 44
Customer 36, 145, 149, 151, 152,
        155-176, 201, 202, 216

D

Design 230, 231, 233, 236-238
Diet 29-31, 131-138, 141-143
Disability 197, 199, 200

E

Education 33-35, 37, 38, 41, 44
Employee 112, 115-117, 119-121, 123,
        126, 127
Employees 53, 65, 78, 79, 80
Employer 112, 118, 120-122, 126
Expense 203
Experience 111, 114, 115, 122, 124,
        182, 186

F

Fat 133, 135-138, 141, 143

Feedback 149-152
Fines 104
Food 20, 21, 24, 25, 27-32, 100-105,
    107-109, 112-114, 120, 123, 126,
    147, 148, 150, 151, 153

H

Health 131-134, 138, 139, 141, 142
Hire 111-113, 116-118, 126-128

I

Images 230, 232
Ingredients 184-186
Insurance 197-200
Interview 119
Investment 14, 15
IRA 198

K

Keywords 215-218, 220-227
Kitchen 13, 24, 25, 27-29, 57, 86-88,
    91, 93, 94, 97, 98, 100-109, 184,
    257, 260, 262

L

Learn 34-37, 40, 43, 44
License 106

M

Marketing 184, 201, 202, 217, 218
Meal 45, 49, 52, 62, 71, 76, 79-81
Meetings 42, 43
Menu 60, 62
Money 83, 84, 86, 88

O

Opportunity 167, 168, 178
Option 52, 71
Options 136
Owner 197, 198, 200

P

Pay 182, 183, 186, 187

Positive 170
Prepare 19, 24, 25, 27, 31, 100-102,
    104, 106, 109, 150
Pricing 181, 182, 183, 185, 188, 190
Problem 155, 161, 163, 166, 167, 169,
    171, 174, 175
Product 57, 60, 61, 64
Professional 102, 108
Profit 53, 54, 56, 66, 67, 79, 83, 85, 181,
    182, 183, 229, 250
Promotional Offers 52, 55

Q

Quality 111, 112, 128
Questions 113-115, 119-122, 125-127,
    129, 145, 146, 149-152

R

Recipe 13
Responsibility 198
Restaurant 14, 15, 34, 43
Review 26

S

Satisfaction 146, 151, 152, 156
Self-employed 197, 200
Service 34, 43, 48, 51-54, 56, 59, 63,
    65, 70, 71, 73, 84, 102, 104, 155,
    158, 160-164, 167-172, 174-176,
    184, 186-188, 190, 201-203, 206,
    224-226
Software 207, 208, 222, 223, 232, 233,
    234, 238, 242, 250-254
Staff 112, 118, 126
Storage 98, 102, 103
Strategy 46, 56, 58-60
Success 45-47, 56, 60, 194
Supplies 63, 67-69, 83, 86, 93
Survey 101, 102, 145, 146, 152

W

Web site 202-212, 214-227, 230-253